BRITAIN'S
BEST
Bakery

BRITAIN'S BEST Bakery

Over 100 recipes inspired by the best bakeries in Britain

with Mich Turner & Peter Sidwell

NEW HOLLAND

Contents

Speciality Bakes 14

NORTH WEST ENGLAND AND SCOTLAND 17

Afternoon Tea 258

Introduction

Britain is a nation that loves to bake and we Brits are good at it too. Who doesn't love a rich and flaky pastry bun, liberally sprinkled with crunchy sugar and generously filled with plump fruit, or a soft, light-as-air sponge flavoured with a shot of coffee and lavishly topped with cream and crunchy walnuts? Baking is part of our heritage. Not only do we love to bake, we love to share a treat too. And Britain's bakeries are keen to share their produce with us. Whether artisan sourdoughs, bespoke special occasion confections, or everyday cakes, traybakes and pastries that transport us in

a nostalgic instant back to our childhood memories, Britain is a bakery loving nation.

And with such an abundance of bakeries, how would we find Britain's best? The nationwide search began in earnest. Hundreds of applicants were whittled down to just 60 bakeries, each representing five designated regions of the British Isles. This diverse group of independent, family-run or community bakeries brought to the competition skilled artisans, master bakers, more used to judging the skills of others than being assessed themselves, champion pie-makers, specialist pâtisseries, award-winning cake makers, cupcake specialists and confident Michelin-star chefs, all looking to win the title of Britain's Best Bakery.

Among the competing bakeries were those with a social conscience, that reached out to their communities and offered the opportunity to learn practical as well as social skills. There were young people just starting out with a clear vision, a strong sense of purpose and the drive and passion to succeed in business. Their enthusiasm was infectious, and just as likely to be shared by bakers with a lifetime of baking experience as the newcomers to the field. We found second, third and fourth generation bakers who retained a passion for their products and the ingredients they sourced to make them. Some competitors had started cottage industries, working from their home kitchens and steadily increasing their customer base until they could take on premises and staff and invest in their futures. Others were trained specially and served apprenticeships, or had travelled the world honing their skills, as well as developing their palates and storing up recipes and flavour combinations to serve later to loyal customers. Surprisingly many of our bakers were self-taught, learning their trade on the job, or people who had turned a pleasing hobby into a fledgling business when their circumstances allowed.

There were experimental bakers among their number: those who loved to tinker with a flavour combination, who measured ingredient quantities by eye and feel as well as those who were exact, weighing out precise quantities and never deviating from a successful recipe.

The array of products offered for sale from our contestants was vast. From sourdough loaves made using long fermentation methods that develop the bread's flavour and character, to mass produced oven-bottom baked breads. We tested every offering assessing them for flavour, taste, texture, presentation and skill. We wanted each to showcase the best of their region but retain their own distinct

identity. Some had already overcome that challenge. There were bakeries that served only vegetarian foods, those who specialised in food intolerances, a bakery that milled its own flour, one that loved to forage for its ingredients for free and another that was almost entirely self-sufficient in sourcing the ingredients it put into its bakes. Some made recipes that were more than 100 years old and using methods our distant ancestors would recognise, while others made innovative use of ingredients that are newly available, or took inspiration from French, American or Australian cuisine.

Whatever their starting point, the competition intended to pit the best bakeries against each other in a series of challenges that would put their skills and techniques, ingenuity and craftsmanship and ultimately, their palates, to the test.

In meeting the contestants, Britain's Best Bakery *revealed fascinating stories about our nation, its history and our eating preferences through the pastries, breads and cakes that were presented to the judges. Who knew that Cumberland rum nicky incorporated expensive spices fresh from the thriving northern port of Whitehaven and was made to be served to sailors?*

Or that Eccles cakes could be improved upon and turned into the unique Rossendale cakes, or that sourdough traditionally made incorporates some of yesterday's uncooked dough, that had now turned sour?

To celebrate the achievements of this batch of bakeries, the best recipes inspired by the series are included here for you to make at home. The Speciality Bakes chapter introduces each of the 60 bakeries that took part in the five regional competitions together with a recipe from each that represents the jewel in their bakery's crown, while the Afternoon Tea chapter presents 40 delicious sweet and savoury recipes that are perfect for making and serving at any time.

Judges

MICH TURNER MBE

Mich Turner had a keen interest in food from child-hood, winning a Devon school's cookery competition at the age of 15. Her passion turned practical and she graduated from university with a degree in food science and nutrition in 1992. From there she went on to work as a pâtisserie buyer at world-renown luxury goods store Harvey Nichols, until she set up Little Venice Cake Company in 1999. Since then she has become an authority on bakery and creative cake décoration, successfully combining her scientific knowledge and understanding of baking with her creative and artistic talent to design show-stopping cakes. In her career she has made and decorated cakes for royalty and many A-list celebrities. Little Venice Cake Company has become an award-winning company. Mich is the author of several best-selling books on the subject of cake decorating. She regularly hosts international masterclasses and is a guest speaker and demonstrator at events, shows and exhibitions. Recently she launched a range of bakeware and cake decorating tools. Mich was Harper's Bazaar and Chanel Entrepreneur of the Year in 2006, and received an MBE in The Queen's Birthday Honours 2010.

PETER SIDWELL

Peter Sidwell trained as a chef in Yorkshire and spent 20 years honing his craft in some of the best hotels in Europe with a passion for artisan baking. He then went on to work in corporate catering for an international bank. Later he made a life-changing decision to go it alone opening Simply Good Taste, writing a series of internally best-selling cook books and running a cookery school. In 2010, Peter's first television series Lakes on a Plate was aired. It was a celebration of his passion for the Lake District and its food and received great reviews. In January 2012, he opened Peter Sidwell@rheged cafe at Cumbria's Rheged Centre specialising in re-creating modern Britich classic dishes . Peter is becoming a regular face at food festivals, exhibitions and demos, packing out theatres with his relaxed and enthusiastic approach to his food, ingredients and artisan baking.

The Recipes: Before You Begin

Many of the recipes included in this book are quick and easy to make and so delicious that they may become a regular part of your baking repertoire. Others are spectacular creations that you may choose to make for a special celebration, requiring more time and patience in the making, and even needing specialist ingredients that you may have to source online. As with all recipes, preparation is key. Before you begin, read the recipe through and make sure you understand all of the instructions before you start.

Some of the artisan breads incorporate a 'starter' into the recipe. Although these can be purchased online, or even be purchased from a bakery, you can make your own, and it can be a fun part of the process. If this is your choice then advance planning is key. Some of the starters may take several days to prepare before you can even begin to make a loaf of bread, though once made, if looked after and nurtured, a good starter will last for years. The recipe on the right-hand page will be suitable for any of the recipes mentioned in this book.

Make sure you have all the ingredients to hand before you begin. There's nothing worse than starting to bake and realising midway through the course of the recipe that you don't quite have enough of an ingredient. Always buy the best quality ingredients that you can afford, the results of your baking endeavours will prove their worth.

Eggs: medium eggs are used unless otherwise stated.
Butter: unsalted butter is preferred for baking, unless otherwise stated.
Chocolate: buy milk, plain (semi-sweet) or dark (bittersweet) according to preference, though chocolate that contains a larger quantity of cocoa solids is considered to be better quality and will have a purer taste.

BAKEWARE

Bakeware is a significant investment. If you're new to baking then it may take time to work out which key pieces of equipment you should invest in. Good bakeware is rigid, will not buckle in the oven under extreme temperatures and will conduct heat evenly and efficiently. If cared for correctly, it will last a lifetime. Typical first purchases will ideally include a couple of round springform cake tins (pans), a muffin or cupcake mould and a couple of sturdy baking sheets.

The largest piece of kit is your oven. All ovens vary in terms of how they conduct heat, how long they take to reach the required temperature and how well they retain their heat. Fan ovens should have an even temperature throughout, but conventional ovens are usually hotter at the top than they are at the bottom. As a guide, bake food in the centre of the oven and if you are baking two or more items spaced on shelves stacked directly above each other, then it's a good idea to switch their baking positions part way through the bake. Ensure that the oven rails are level. If you can, test the temperature of your oven with an oven thermometer. If you bake with a fan oven you may need to reduce the temperature by as much as 20 degrees.–

WEIGHING AND MEASURING

Measurements for the recipes are given in metric and imperial. Choose one of these measures and stick to it throughout. The measurements are not interchangeable.

1 teaspoon = 5 ml
1 tablespoon = 15 ml

Peter Sidwell's Sourdough Starter

INGREDIENTS

350 g (12 oz) strong white bread flour, plus extra for dusting
350 ml (12 fl oz) water

Day 1: Put 100 g (3½ oz) of the strong white bread flour and 100 ml (3½ fl oz) water into a bowl and mix together with your hands to form a batter. Leave the bowl out in the open overnight to encourage the yeast spores to develop, which will make for a better and stronger fermentation.

Day 2: Add 50 g (1¾ oz) the remaining flour and 50 ml (1¾ fl oz) of the remaining water, then mix together, cover and place in the refrigerator. You should start to see bubbles forming and a slight sour smell to the mixture.

Day 3: Add 50 g (1¾ oz) the remaining flour and 50 ml (1¾ fl oz) of the remaining water, then mix together, cover and place in the refrigerator.

Day 4: Add 50 g (1¾ oz) the remaining flour and 50 ml (1¾ fl oz) of the remaining water, then mix together, cover and place in the refrigerator.

Day 5: Add 50 g (1¾ oz) the remaining flour and 50 ml (1¾ fl oz) of the remaining water, then mix together, cover and place in the refrigerator.

Day 6: Add in the remaining flour and water, then mix together, cover and place in the refrigerator.

Keep feeding the remaining sourdough starter every couple of days with equal amounts of flour and water as detailed above, then it will be ready for the next loaf.

Speciality Bakes

Each of the 60 bakeries that was selected to take part in the competition is introduced in this chapter, which is organised according to region. A biography of each bakery is presented along with the recipe that, for them, represents the best that their bakery has to offer. For judge Peter Sidwell, this is the product that has the customers queuing to buy more. It's the stand-out bake that is sold in hundred or thousands each week. For some that means good old-fahioned pies, puddings and cakes. For others it might be an artisan sourdough, or a special occasion gateau. Whether it's a dish specific to the region, a baked good that pays homage to the baker's ancestry, or a hand-me-down recipe, these are the bakes that we love to eat.

North West England and Scotland

Birdhouse Bakery, Muthill, Perthshire

Bakers
Suzanne (Owner) and Susan (Assistant)

Size of Business
1 shop, 6 staff

Type of Business
Boutique bakery and tea room

Suzanne fell in love with baking when she was pregnant, but the idea for a shop came later once her children started school. Each time she walked past this empty shop and looked inside at the derelict space she always thought what a great shop it would make. Her vision became the Birdhouse Bakery. The bakery is based on what Suzanne calls, 'a mother's kitchen'. No additives are ever used in the baked goods. Suzanne wants a chance to show that it's possible to achieve success in a tiny village.

Although a new business and set in a remote location, Birdhouse Bakery has received some superb reviews on the internet. Assistant Susan, began working at the bakery after being made redundant from a job she'd held for 20 years.

The bakery is based on what Suzanne calls 'a Mother's kitchen'.

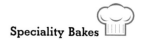

Carrot Cake

MAKES 1 CAKE

SPONGE

175 g (6 oz) dark brown sugar

3 eggs

150 ml (¼ pint) sunflower oil

200 g (7 oz) self-raising (self-rising) flour

1 teaspoon bicarbonate of soda (baking soda)

3 teaspoons mixed (apple pie) spice

Zest of 1 large orange

200 g (7 oz) carrots, peeled and coarsely grated

110 g (4 oz) sultanas (golden raisins)

50 g (1¾ oz) desiccated (unsweetened, shredded) coconut

50 g (1¾ oz) pecans or walnuts, roughly chopped

FROSTING

200 g (7 oz) unsalted French butter, softened

400 g (14 oz) icing (confectioners') sugar, sifted

2 tablespoons milk

¼ teaspoon vanilla extract

250 g (9 oz) full-fat cream cheese

1 teaspoon ground cinnamon

50 g (1¾ oz) pecans or walnuts, to decorate

SYRUP GLAZE

Juice from the large orange

1 tablespoon lemon juice

75 g (2½ oz) dark brown sugar

Preheat the oven to 170°C/310°F/Gas mark 3½. Grease and line two 20 cm (8 in) round cake tins (pans).

SPONGE

In a bowl, whisk the sugar, eggs and oil together with a hand whisk for 2 minutes, or until the sugar has dissolved. Sift over the flour, bicarbonate of soda and mixed spice and stir in gently. Add in the rest of the ingredients and mix gently. Divide the batter between the prepared cake tins. Bake for 30 minutes. Remove from the oven and leave to set for a few minutes before turning out onto a wire rack.

FROSTING

Meanwhile, to make the frosting, in a bowl, beat the butter and sifted icing sugar. Warm the milk and vanilla in a microwave, or in a saucepan over gentle heat on the stove, then add to the butter and icing sugar mixture. Whisk together until light and fluffy then fold in the cream cheese. Gently mix in the cinnamon, taking care not to over-whisk.

SYRUP GLAZE

To make the syrup glaze, pour the orange and lemon juices into a small saucepan with the sugar and heat gently over a low heat until the sugar has dissolved. Spike the cakes all over with a skewer and pour the glaze over the top of each while warm. Leave to cool.

Put one cake on a serving plate, top with a third of the frosting then top with the other sponge. Smooth the remaining frosting over the top of the cake and decorate with pecans or walnuts.

The Wee Boulangerie, Edinburgh

Bakers
Katia Lebart (Head Baker) and Sharon Iacono
(Assistant)

Size of Business
1 shop, 2 bakers, 6 staff

Type of Bakery
Artisan bakery selling breads, baguettes
and pastries

The Wee Boulangerie sells traditional products with a French twist, all influenced by the food and tastes of head baker Katia's native France. The Edinburgh-based artisan bakery is particularly proud of its baguettes, focaccias, brioches, rye bread, macarons and nougat. Customers are known to queue to buy Katia's signature bakes fresh from the oven. She believes in traditional baking methods that use very long fermentations to develop the flavours and characteristics of the breads, and always uses flours with no additives or improvers. Katia draws on her strong, childhood memories and experience of food to inspire her bread baking.

Though a formally trained baker, Katia's first career was as a lecturer in engineering, but her passion for food won out and she retrained.

The Wee Boulangerie sells traditional products with a French twist. They are particularly proud of their baguettes, focaccias, brioches and rye bread, and also their macarons and nougat.

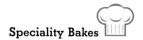

Fougasse

MAKES 2

DOUGH

170 g (5½ oz) strong white bread flour
30 g (1 oz) wholemeal (whole-wheat) flour
Generous pinch of salt
2–3 g fresh yeast
30 ml (1 fl oz) water
4 teaspoons olive oil

FILLING

100 g (3½ oz) Cheddar, grated (shredded)
50 g (1¾ oz) bacon lardons, fried

DOUGH

To make the dough, put all the ingredients, except for the cheese and bacon in an electric mixer fitted with a dough hook and mix together to form a dough, about 7 minutes. Put the dough in a clean bowl and set aside to prove for about 2 hours at room temperature, until doubled in size. Preheat the oven to 230°C/450°F/Gas mark 8.

Divide the dough into 2 equal pieces. Flatten slightly and leave to rest on wooden planks.

FILLING

Flatten the breads slightly with the tips of the fingers. Spread the fillings in the middle and enclose the dough around them. Shape the bread into baguettes, cut the surface with scissors and put onto baking sheets. Bake for 15 minutes, turn out onto a wire rack and leave to cool.

Murrays, Perth

Owner/Bakers
Linda (Owner) and Colin (Bakery Manager)

Type of Bakery
Fourth-generation family bakery

Size of Business
1 shop, 18 staff

Murrays pies are 'an institution in Perth,' says bakery owner, Linda, who is the fourth generation of her family to own and run the business. Opened by her great-grandfather in 1901, the bakery passed to her gran and then to her father, before she took the reins. Surprisingly though, Linda isn't the baker, choosing instead to look after the customers in a front-of-house role. The bakery has a very loyal customer base with rave internet reviews about the produce. One man travels in from Manchester to buy dozens of pies at a time and it seems he is not alone in coveting the produce of this bakery.

Many of the recipes made by the bakery have stood the test of time, and been passed down the generations, though contemporary products, such as millionaire's shortbread, have been introduced to attract a younger generation.

The bakery uses local produce and for this reason, some of the baked goods are seasonal.

Pineapple tarts

MAKES 12

PASTRY
75 g (2½ oz) caster (superfine) sugar
150 g (5 oz) margarine
2 large eggs
250 g (9 oz) plain (all-purpose) flour
1 x 400 g (14 oz) can crushed pineapple

MERINGUE FILLING
2 egg whites (at room temperature)
115 g (4 oz) caster (superfine) sugar

FONDANT
500 g (1 lb 2 oz) fondant
1 teaspoon pineapple flavouring
Yellow food colouring

Preheat the oven to 180°C/350°F/Gas mark 4.

PASTRY
In a mixing bowl, beat the sugar and margarine until light and fluffy. Beat in the eggs, then add the flour until it all comes together and comes away from the sides of the bowl. Turn out the dough onto a clean work surface and divide into 12 equal balls. Put into large cupcake size moulds and press to fill the base and sides.

Line the base of each tart with crushed pineapple, then bake for 15–20 minutes, or until golden. Set aside to cool (but not to go cold). Remove the tart shells from their moulds and set aside to cool.

MERINGUE FILLING
To make the filling, put the egg whites into a clean, grease-free bowl and whisk to a medium peak. Add a spoonful of the sugar to the meringue and whisk really hard until all the sugar has dissolved and the mixture starts to look shiny. Add the remaining sugar gradually, whisking continually until the mixture becomes really shiny and very stiff (it should not fall off the spoon when lifted). Fill the cool tarts with the meringue mix.

FONDANT
Place the fondant in a pan and heat gently until very soft. Add the pineapple flavouring and a little yellow food colouring. Dip each tart into fondant to coat the top. Leave until set.

Murrays pies are an 'institution in Perth,' says owner Linda.

The Muffin Top Boutique Bakery, Whitehaven, Cumbria

Owner/Baker
Sarah Lithgow (Owner) and Kirsty Davidson (Assistant)

Type of Bakery
Celebration cake shop and baking equipment and partyware specialist

Size of Business
1 shop, 2 staff

Baking cupcakes was a lifeline for Sarah Lithgow, who found herself in daunting circumstances when husband Stuart was made redundant back in 2010. 'We were so short of money, I started making cupcakes from home and selling them at a Christmas market.' Interest grew after she displayed her cakes on Facebook and Sarah has been baking ever since.

This beautiful boutique cake shop opened its doors back in September 2012. It is here that Sarah makes her bespoke celebration cakes to order. Sarah ensures that all her cakes are a one-of-a-kind creation, whether it's for a birthday or a 10-tier wedding cake. 'I try not to make the same cake twice. There's nothing more rewarding than the look on a customer's face, when they see their cake', she says.

Sarah has learnt her skills on the job. 'I'll be honest,' she says, 'I Google videos of how to do things, use my vast selection of cookbooks and also learn as I go. I'm still learning.'

The bakery opens just three days a week, selling flapjacks, cupcakes, brownies, gingerbread and scones. Sarah opens the doors at 11.30 am and stays open until she's sold everything, which proudly, she admits, doesn't take long. A lot of Sarah's recipes have been passed to her by her mother and grandmothers and are also a result of experimentation. Sarah does all the baking herself. 'I hand make some things and use mixers, although pastry is always handmade just as my grandma taught me,' she says. Her new employee Kirsty runs the shop, while husband Stuart helps out behind the scenes.

Sarah says, the bakery 'proves that sometimes a pipe dream can become reality and can actually make a real difference, not only to us as a family, but also the community. The shop is, in my opinion, a little jewel in the town. Whitehaven has recently suffered some terrible times, but the support from the local community is fantastic. I feel very privileged to call West Cumbria home'.

'I try not to make the same cake twice. There is nothing more rewarding than the look on a customer's face, when they see their cake.'

Strawberry Vanilla Birthday Cake

MAKES 1 CAKE

SPONGE

340 g (11¾ oz) unsalted butter, plus extra for greasing

340 g (11¾ oz) caster (superfine) sugar

6 eggs

340 g (11¾ oz) self-raising (self-rising) flour

FROSTING AND TOPPING

300 g (11 oz) unsalted butter

600 g (1 lb 6 oz) icing (confectioners') sugar, plus extra for dusting

2 teaspoons vanilla extract

370 g (13 oz) good-quality strawberry jam

15 fresh strawberries, halved

1 kg (2¼ lb) fondant

Preheat the oven to 180°C/350°F/Gas mark 4. Grease and line two 23 cm (9 in) round cake tins (pans).

SPONGE

To make the sponge, cream the butter and sugar in a large mixing bowl until light and fluffy. Add 3 of the eggs and half of the flour and beat until combined. Repeat with the rest of the eggs and flour. Divide the mixture between the prepared tins and bake for 20–25 minutes, until the sponge is golden on top and it bounces back when you press it in the centre. Leave to set for a few minutes before turning out on to a wire rack to go cold.

FROSTING

To make the frosting, beat together the butter, icing sugar and vanilla extract in a food processor or blender. If the batter is a little stiff, add a drop of boiling water to loosen the mixture slightly.

Trim the top of both cakes level. Arrange one sponge on a serving plate trimmed side up, top with half of the frosting, all the strawberry jam and strawberry halves. Place the other cake on top, trimmed side down, to create a flat cake surface, then coat the sides and top with the rest of the frosting. Dip a palette knife in boiling water before smoothing the icing to create a professional finish. Refrigerate for 20 minutes to keep the cake firm.

TOPPING

Meanwhile, knead the fondant until soft and pliable on a surface lightly dusted with icing sugar. Roll it out to 3 mm (¹/₈ in) thick. Use to cover the cake and smooth the surface.

Appleby Bakery, Appleby-in-Westmorland, Cumbria

Owners/Bakers
Jackie Kirkpatrick and Carol Thornton (Owners) and Tracey Pearson (Bakery Manager) and Sarah Kirkpatrick (Baker)

Type of Bakery
Traditional Cumbrian bakery, popular with the tourist trade

Size of Business
2 shops, 20 staff

This award-winning bakery, named for the town with the old world charm in which it trades, sells traditional and regional products made 'using the same methods that Cumbrian housewives have used for years,' according to owner Jackie.

This is a bakery with a wholesale operation. Baked goods are produced off site and sold into farm shops, delis and Booths, the local independent supermarket. The wholesale range includes 10 traditional cakes, 8 traybakes and a Christmas selection.

Appleby Bakery makes a mixture of old recipes passed on from relatives, as well as Cumbrian and traditional WI recipes. The bakery's best-selling recipe for very sticky ginger cake (they sell three times more of this product than anything else) originates from a 1957 local parish WI recipe book that belonged to Jackie's mother. This recipe together with their traditional Cumbrian Borrowdale teabread and Cumbrian rum nicky have helped them win 8 Gold Taste Awards over the last 3 years.

Back in the 1750s, Whitehaven was the second largest port in England. Slaves and spices from the Indies were traded there, and as a result the regional recipes contain plenty of aromatic spices as well as flavourful molasses. Sailors were paid their bonuses in goods, and Cumbrian rum nicky (the recipe is featured here) was developed for them. If the cooks didn't have enough ingredients, they 'nicked' the rest, which is why it is called a rum nicky, says Jackie.

The recipe for their sticky ginger cake originates from a 1957 local parish WI recipe book that belonged to Jackie's mother.

Cumberland Rum Nicky

MAKES 1 TART

PASTRY

250 g (9 oz) plain (all-purpose) flour, plus extra for dusting
75 g (2½ oz) icing (confectioners') sugar
2 egg yolks
Zest of 1 orange
2 tablespoons rum
150 g (5 oz) butter, softened

FILLING

200 g (7 oz) dates
85 g (3 oz) sultanas (golden raisins)
50 g (1¾ oz) stem ginger, pulped
1 apple, pulped
70 g (2½ oz) light brown sugar
6 tablespoons rum
140 g (4¾ oz) butter, melted
1 egg, lightly beaten
60 g (2 oz) brown sugar

Preheat the oven to 170°C/310°F/Gas mark 3½.

PASTRY

To make the pastry, mix together the flour, icing sugar, egg yolks, orange zest and rum in a large bowl. Add the melted butter and beat until the mixture binds together. Use two-thirds of the pastry to line a flan tin, 20 x 30 cm (8 x 12 in).

FILLING

To make the filling, in a bowl, combine the dates, sultanas, ginger, apple, brown sugar and rum. Mix in the melted butter. Tip on top of the pastry and push to the edges to make an even covering.

Roll out the remaining pastry on a lightly floured surface, and cut into strips. Cover the flan filling with a lattice design.
Mix together the beaten egg and brown sugar. Use to brush the top of the pastry. This will give the top a golden crunch.
Bake for 25–30 minutes, or until golden brown.

Crags Country Bakery, Carlisle

Owner/Bakers
Ron Garrigle and son Craig

Type of Bakery
Family-run artisan bakery selling bread and cake

Speciality Bake
Crags bread (their take on a traditional fruit bread), carrot cake and sticky toffee cupcakes

This family-run artisan bakery was set up two years ago by former restaurant chef Ron, and son Craig, a trained pâtisserie chef. Baking duties are shared out equally, with Ron being responsible for baking the bread while Craig concentrates on making and decorating the cakes and gateaux.

Ron's working day starts at midnight. He bakes his breads through the night so that they're ready to sell first thing in the morning. They pride themselves on their unique artisan bread and their variety of their sophisticated special occasion cakes.

Most popular breads include chia, corn, olive, and treacle, while carrot cake and sticky toffee cupcakes are the most popular. Their ingredients are sourced from their local wholesalers.

Their recipes are developed through lots of 'trial and error', though they love being challenged to create new bakes by their local customer base.

They pride themselves on their unique artisan bread and their variety of sophisticated cakes for every occasion.

Crags Bread

MAKES 1

STARTER
600 ml (1 pint) milk
230 g (8¼ oz) strong white bread flour

BREAD DOUGH
100 g (3½ oz) yeast
Pinch of sugar
1 kg (2 lb 4 oz) strong white bread flour

10 g (⅓ oz) salt
150 g (5 oz) sugar, plus extra for dusting
50 g (1¾ oz) butter
30 g (1 oz) mixed (apple pie) spice
100 ml (3½ fl oz) whisky
400 g (14 oz) sultanas (golden raisins)
300 g (11 oz) raisins
300 g (11 oz) currants
1 egg, lightly beaten, for glazing

STARTER
To make the starter, warm the milk in a pan over medium heat to blood temperature (about 32°C/89°F). In a mixing bowl, thoroughly mix the flour and yeast with the warm milk. Use a hand blender, if you have one. Set aside for 1–1½ hours.

BREAD DOUGH
Pour the starter into the bowl of an electric mixer, add the remaining ingredients and mix for 6–10 minutes on medium speed. If the mixture is a little dry add a little more milk. Cover and leave to prove until doubled in volume.

Weigh 500 g (1 lb 2 oz) of the dough and put in a panettone mould and set on a bread stone then leave to double in size.

Preheat the oven to 200°C/400°F/Gas mark 6. Glaze the top of the dough with egg and sprinkle with sugar. Bake for 50 minutes to 1 hour. Turn out onto a wire rack and leave to go cold.

Lilibets of Paris, Southport

Owner/Bakers
Lilibet (Elizabeth) Connard and Charlie Nicklin
(Assistant)

Type of Bakery
French pâtisserie, bespoke wedding and
celebration cakes

Size of Business
1 shop, 2 staff

At just 13 years of age Lilibet made it through to the quarter finals of the television series Junior MasterChef. The experience gave her an exciting glimpse of what it would be like to work with food. Upon graduating from university though, Lilibet moved to Paris to master the language she had studied and in doing so cultivated a love of French food. She soon went to train at Le Cordon Bleu Culinary School in Paris, where she excelled in her year group. Her next move was to return to the seaside resort of her upbringing to open her own quaint and visually enticing pâtisserie.

Lilibet and assistant Charlie bake everything by hand in a large open-plan kitchen where they can be watched by their customers. She sources as many of her ingredients as possible from France including butter, flour and chocolate. Lilibet is a stickler for perfection and truly believes her baking skills are 'second to none'.

The recipes she uses are a mixture of family favourites, traditional French pâtisserie and experimental ideas, each appealing to her loyal and varied spectrum of customers.

The company has supplied exclusive store Fortnum and Mason with a bespoke handmade range of iced gingerbread.

Lilibets of Paris were finalists in Southport Food & Drink Festival, in the 'Southport Gem' category.

Lilibet and assistant Charlie bake everything by hand in a large open-plan kitchen where they can be watched by their customers.

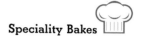

Fraisier

. . . .

MAKES 1 CAKE

SPONGE
150 g eggs (approximately 3)
50 g egg yolk (approximately 3½)
125 g (4¼ oz) caster (superfine) sugar
25 g (1 oz) unsalted French butter
125 g (4¼ oz) T55 flour, or plain (all-purpose) flour, sifted twice)

MOUSSELINE CREAM
1 Madagascan vanilla pod (bean)
300 ml (½ pint) whole milk

60 g egg yolks (approximately 4)
95 g (3¾ oz) caster (superfine) sugar
25 g (1 oz) plain (all-purpose) flour
25 g (1 oz) cornflour (corn starch)
160 g (5¼ oz) unsalted French butter, chilled and diced

ITALIAN MERINGUE
50 ml (2 fl oz) water
150 g (5 oz) caster (superfine) sugar
50 egg whites (approximately 1½)
400 g (14 oz) strawberries

Preheat the oven to 170°C/310°C/Gas mark 3½. Grease and line two 18 cm (7 in) cake tins (pans).

SPONGE
In a large bowl, whisk the eggs and egg yolks with the sugar until light and a figure of eight will hold. Melt the butter in a pan over medium heat. Add some whisked eggs to the pan to combine, while whisking continuously, then pour the butter mixture into the whisked eggs, and fold to combine. Sift in the flour and carefully fold to combine. Pour into the prepared tins and bake for approximately 20 minutes, or until the centre springs back when touched. When cool, remove from the tin.

MOUSSELINE CREAM
Split the vanilla pod in half and scrape out the seeds. Heat the milk in a pan over medium heat with the vanilla seeds and pod and bring to the boil. Meanwhile, put the egg yolks in a bowl with the sugar, flour and cornflour and whisk together. Remove the vanilla pod using a slotted spoon and pour some of the milk into the bowl containing the egg and sugar mixture, whisk and return to the pan. Whisk continuously until it starts to thicken and as soon as it bubbles once, remove from the heat and incorporate the butter until smooth. Cover with cling film (plastic wrap) and leave to cool, then refrigerate.

MERINGUE
Heat the water and sugar in a pan over medium heat until it reaches a 'soft boil' at 112–113°C/233–235°F. Whisk the egg whites in a clean, grease-free bowl, until stiff and then pour in the soft boil sugar and continue to whisk until cool.

Line an 18 cm (7 in) mousse mould with milar (a plastic acetate available from specialist kitchen suppliers) and place on a board. Part fill a piping bag with the cream and pipe a circle of the cream on the board so it is touching the milar. Slice a round from the genoise sponge and place in the mould so that it just touches the piped cream. Slice the strawberries in half and arrange around the edges of the mould with the cut face of the strawberries facing outward. Pipe mousseline cream on top of the sponge and into the gaps. Fill the centre with chopped strawberries and mousseline cream. Top with another layer of sponge and pipe mousseline cream around the edge and crown with Italian meringue.

Cissy Green's Bakery, Rossendale, Lancashire

Owner/Bakers
Barry Haworth

Size of Business
1 shop, 10 staff

Type of Bakery
Traditional bakery selling meat pies, pasties,
breads and cakes

'Cissy Green' was the daughter of the original nineteenth-century bakery owners, and her ghost is well known to the staff. The bakehouse, in the basement, is almost 200 years old and is home to the original coal-burning ovens as well as more 'modern' Victorian ones. Owner Barry says the bakery is almost like a functioning museum.

Barry is fanatical about keeping old-fashioned bakery skills going, and learnt all he knows from watching other bakers when he took over the business. His mother was a confectioner and he grew up in a bakery. 'Cissy Green is dead and gone', he says 'but some of the recipes that her parents passed on went back way beyond their era. There is history in the methods of making things and I want to carry on that tradition. It's an art to be able to bake properly.'

Former butcher Barry is most passionate about making his famous pies. Not surprisingly he makes them to a recipe that has been legendary in the town for nearly 200 years. But it's not just the meat pies that have proved to be a winner, his bakery also created Rossendale cakes, a kind of elongated Eccles Cake made with dried fruits and spices and once featured on the cover of British Baker magazine.

Winston Churchill is believed to be the shop's most famous customer. Apparently he got lost in the town.

Winston Churchill was believed to be the shop's most famous customer. Apparently he got lost in the town.

Rossendale Cakes

· ·

MAKES 9

PASTRY

400 g (14 oz) plain (all-purpose) flour, plus extra for dusting
Pinch of salt
Pinch of baking powder
225 g (8 oz) butter or margarine
5–6 tablespoons cold water

1 egg, lightly beaten, for the egg wash
sugar, for sprinkling

FILLING

225 g (8 oz) sultanas (golden raisins)
60 g (2 oz) glacé cherries, finely chopped
¼ teaspoon mixed (apple pie) spice
¼ teaspoon ground nutmeg
60 g (2 oz) brown sugar
30 g (1 oz) butter
30 ml (generous 1 fl oz) liquid glucose
60 g (2 oz) cake crumb from a stale cake

PASTRY

To make the pastry, put the flour, salt and baking powder in large bowl and then rub in the fat using your fingertips until the mixture resembles fine breadcrumbs. Add the water slowly. Mix with a fork until the dough comes together. Knead a little, then wrap in cling film (plastic wrap) and refrigerate for 20 minutes.

Preheat the oven to 190°C/375°F/Gas mark 5.

FILLING

In a large bowl, combine all the ingredients for the fruit and spice mixture. Cut the pastry into 9 equal pieces and roll out on a lightly floured surface. Divide the fruit and spice mixture between each pastry round, fold the edges over (to make a purse) and pinch the edges together gently. Turn the purses over, squash slightly with the heel of the hand and roll into an oval shape. Brush with egg wash and sprinkle sugar on top. Bake for 15 minutes, or until the pastry is cooked through and golden.

Elizabeth May, Chorley, Lancashire

Owner/Bakers
Susan Elizabeth Millar and Margaret May

Type of Bakery
Special occasion cake retailer

Size of Business
1 shop, 2 staff.

This mother and daughter duo are self-taught bakers and sugarcraft artists who strive for perfection in their edible masterpieces. Mum Margaret had reached an age where she was hoping to retire, rather than starting up a new business with her daughter.

The business was established in 2009 and the shop opened in December 2011. It has a quaint vintage parlour feel with an open-plan kitchen, and according to Susan and Margaret feels as if it is the hub of the local community. They also have an online shop selling brownies, cakes, and novelties, such as chocolate shoes and meerkats.

Together they make all their products on site without the use of preservatives or emulsifiers. Susan is the creative force while Margaret does the majority of the baking. Both can turn their hands to all types of baking and love researching new flavour combinations. They are also chocolatiers and will cover and decorate cakes in chocolate to specification.

In 2013 at the County Brides' Awards they won the North West Best Cake Designer award.

This mother and daughter duo are self-taught bakers and sugarcraft artists who always strive for perfection in their edible masterpieces!

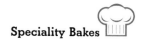

Cake Pops

* *

MAKES ABOUT 30

CAKE

125 g (4¼ oz) butter
150 g (5 oz) caster (superfine) sugar
2 large eggs
Vanilla extract (or flavour of your choice)
150 g (5 oz) self-raising (self-rising) flour
60 ml (2¼ fl oz) milk

DECORATION

70 g (2¼ oz) butter
225 g (8 oz) icing (confectioners') sugar
1 tablespoon milk (optional)
Lollipop (popsicle) sticks
400 g (14 oz) each Belgian chocolate (white, milk or dark)
Edible food colouring (optional)

Preheat the oven 170°C/310°F/Gas mark 3½. Grease and line a 15 cm (6 in) cake tin (pan).

CAKE

In a large mixing bowl, cream the butter and sugar together until pale and smooth, about 2–3 minutes using an electric mixer. In another bowl, beat the eggs with the vanilla, then pour gently into the butter and sugar mixture, a little at a time, and continue to mix for a few minutes after each addition. Sift the flour into another bowl. Add the flour and milk in alternate batches to the butter and sugar mixture, beating well after each addition until all has been incorporated. Tip the batter into the prepared tin and bake for around 30 minutes, or until slightly raised and golden brown. Pierce the centre of the cake with a skewer and if it comes out clean the cake is ready. Leave in the tin to set for 10 minutes before turning out onto a wire rack to go cold.

DECORATION

Meanwhile, to make the decoration, beat the butter in a bowl to soften it. Add the icing sugar and a dash of milk, if needed, and stir to combine. Crumble the cake into a large bowl. Add some of the buttercream and mix together using your hands until it becomes a dough-like texture and you can roll a ball of the mixture. Roll balls of mixture to the size of a golf ball and place on a flat surface. Break a few chunks of chocolate into a small bowl and set over a pan of gently simmering water until melted. Dip 1 cm (³/₈ in) of each lollipop stick in to the melted chocolate and stick one into each cake ball. Freeze until frozen. Melt the rest of the chocolate as before. If you are using white chocolate, colour it with food colour, if you like. Dip each cake ball in the chocolate so that each is fully coated. Stand in foam or polystyrene until set.

Mad Hatters, Chester

· ·

Owner/Bakers
Ann Gardiner and Kerri Elston

Size of Business
2 shops, 15 staff

Type of Bakery
Traditional cakes, scones, petit fours and breads
and afternoon tea

Bakery owners Ann and Kerri used to work as environmental chemists before they started baking professionally and they still have a little bit of the scientist left in them – they love experimenting with traditional, tried-and-tested recipes until they develop their own unique taste. Despite the fact that Ann comes from a family of bakers, both are self-taught, using a huge collection of recipe books and hours of practice to create their products. Their special, quirky creations include Earl Grey cupcakes and vanilla chai Victoria sponge.

Together they opened their first bakery in Chester just three years ago and the business has really taken off. The tearoom and bakery is situated in a historical building (a 350-years-old former rectory) in the city centre, on the city's historical 'Rows'. It was opened by the mayor in April 2011. A new bakery and baking school followed not long after, and in addition the duo have won a string of prestigious awards including Finalist in Business of the Year 2011 (Network She Awards), Bronze in Best Café 2012 (Chester Food & Drink Awards, customer vote), Winner of Coffee Shop of the Year 2012 (Café Trade Award, customer vote), and were National Cupcake Championship finalists in 2013.

All products are made from scratch on the premises. They admit they love challenges from their customers and say they tend to get the interesting orders that other bakeries may refuse to do. Themed afternoon teas, vintage tea parties and baking and decorating classes form part of their repertoire.

Best-selling lines include cupcakes, giant macaroons and double chocolate and raspberry frangipane tarts, and of course, the speciality afternoon teas.

Photograph by Twizzlebird Creative

Although Ann comes from a family of bakers, this duo's skills have been developed thanks to a huge collection of recipe books, hours of practise and lots of experimenting.

Red Berry Tea Cupcakes

MAKES 12 CUPCAKES

SPONGE

4 teaspoons loose-leaf red berry tea
200 ml (7 fl oz) boiling water
150 g (5 oz) butter
150 g (5 oz) sugar
3 eggs
150 g (5 oz) self-raising (self-rising) flour

RASPBERRY COULIS

200 g (7 oz) fresh or frozen raspberries
40 g (1¼ oz) caster (superfine sugar)

RED BERRY TEA BUTTERCREAM

220 g (8 oz) butter
1 kg (2¼ lb) icing (confectioners') sugar
50 ml (2 fl oz) strong red berry tea
White chocolate decorations
12 raspberries, to decorate
12 strawberries, to decorate
Edible glitter, to decorate

SPONGE

Steep the loose-leaf red berry tea in boiling water for at least 15 minutes. Strain 50 ml (2 fl oz) into a measuring cup and allow to cool. Do NOT discard the tea berries or remaining tea.

Preheat the oven to 180°C/350°F/Gas mark 4 and line two trays of muffin cups with paper cases.

Using an electric mixer set to high speed, cream the butter and sugar in a mixing bowl, until light and fluffy. Add the eggs, one at a time, until well incorporated. Add one-third of the flour mix and incorporate, then add one-third of the tea. Repeat twice more, mixing on a slower speed and being careful not to overwork. Chop the tea berries and fold gently into the cake batter using a spatula. Fill each paper case two-thirds full and bake for 20 minutes, or until a skewer inserted into the centre comes out clean. Set aside on a wire rack to go cold. Cut a small cube from the middle of the cold cakes.

RASPBERRY COULIS

Put the raspberries, sugar and two tablespoons of the water into a heavy saucepan. Heat to a gentle simmer and cook for 15 minutes until the fruit has softened and the sugar has dissolved. Remove from the heat and pass through a fine sieve, use the back of a wooden spoon to gently push the fruit through. Set aside and allow to cool.

BUTTERCREAM

To make the buttercream, beat the butter in a mixing bowl to soften. Add half of the icing sugar and mix on a low setting until lightly incorporated then turn the mixer to high and mix until pale and fluffy. Add a little of the tea and mix well. Add the remaining icing sugar, a little at a time, then add more tea until the desired texture is achieved.

Put half a teaspoon of coulis in the cupcake, then part fill a piping bag fitted with a plain nozzle with buttercream and pipe onto the top of each cupcake. Top with fruit and a shard of white chocolate (if using). Finish with a dusting of edible glitter.

Cowburn's Family Bakery, Stockport

Owner/Bakers
Richard (Rick) Cowburn (Owner) and Tom (Apprentice)

Type of Bakery
Artisan baker of breads including sourdoughs, pastries and cakes

Size of Business
1 shop, 5 staff

Rick the owner of Cowburn's Family Bakery, is a self-taught baker, but one with a significant amount of practical experience, since it has been his trade for his entire working life – he began working with pastry when he was just 14 and has been developing his skills and experimenting with recipes ever since.

So passionate about his produce is Rick, that he describes his breads as his 'babies' and alludes to the different stages of the bread-making process in terms of the development of a child's life. Through the teens (when the dough doesn't always behave), to the final bake when it's ready to fly the nest. He works according to traditional, simple methods and keeps his produce, which is all baked on site, seasonal.

According to Rick, the bakery is the hub of the local community and he claims to know all his customers by name.

Rick began working with pastry when he was just 14 and has been developing his skills and experimenting with recipes ever since.

Organic Seed Honey Jenny Wren

MAKES 2 LOAVES

RYE FERMENT
120 g (4 oz) rye flour
120 ml (4 fl oz) cold boiled water

BREAD DOUGH
660 g (1½ lb) strong white bread flour
200 g (7 oz) rye flour

75 g (2½ oz) wholemeal (whole-wheat) flour
75 g (2½ oz) malted grain flour
100 g (3½ oz) mixed seeds, plus, extra for coating
25 g (¾ oz) blossom honey
Cold water, for mixing
200 g (7 oz) rye ferment
15 g (½ oz) salt

RYE FERMENT
To make the rye ferment, mix 40 g (1¾ oz) rye flour and 40 ml cold boiled water in a stainless steel bowl. Cover with cling film (plastic wrap) until it show signs of bubbles (about 24 hours). Add to this another 40 g (1¾ oz) rye flour and 40 ml water. Gently mix, then cover again. Let this bubble and swell for at least 24 hours. On day 3, discard one-third of the flour and water mix. Mix another 40 g (1¾ oz) water and 40 g (1¾ oz) rye flour to the remaining two-thirds and let it ferment and bubble. It should start to smell like beer barm. This three-stage operation should yield 200 g (7 oz) of natural rye ferment.

BREAD DOUGH
To make the loaves, mix together all the flours, seeds and honey with just enough cold water to bind the ingredients, but so it's not too stiff. Mix for about 6 minutes in an electric mixer. Leave to rest for 5 minutes. Add the rye ferment and mix for another 6 minutes. Leave to rest for 5 minutes. Add the salt and knead for 5 minutes. The dough should be smooth and firm but light to the touch. Leave to rest for at least 12 hours in the refrigerator. Tip onto a work surface, flatten into a rectangle and fold the top one-third over the centre third, then the bottom one-third over the centre third. Leave to rest for 5–10 minutes. Cut in half and form into balls. Let it rest again. Roll each into a rectangle and fold as before. Repeat and seal the two edges together, keeping the flat-side down. Gently stretch without tearing to form a ball. Roll in extra seeds, place in a proving basket seam side up and leave to prove overnight or for at least 12 hours to almost double in size.

Put a baking tray containing water in the base of the oven and preheat the oven to 220°C/425°F/Gas mark 7. Slash the top of the bread and bake for 17 minutes on a baking sheet. Reduce the oven temperature to 210°C/410°C/Gas mark 6½. Cover the bread with baking parchment and bake for another 15 minutes.

Ye Olde Pastie Shoppe, Bolton, Lancashire

Owner/Bakers
Marie Walsh (Owner) and Marvin (Baker)

Size of Business
1 shop, 10 staff

Type of Bakery
Traditional pasty shop

This traditional Bolton bakery has been in owner Marie Walsh's family since 1898. She took over the reins in the 1970s and steadfastly refuses to retire. She's also passionate about keeping the bakery true to its roots. This shop has become something of an institution in the town, and a 'must see' attraction according to Marie. Check out any internet reviews and the pasties are universally regarded as magnificent, with customers travelling great distances and prepared to queue to be served their iconic pasty. All the bakers are self-taught and keep to the old, simple traditional recipes, that the locals love. All produce is baked on site by hand and is sourced locally.

Marie's pasty shop boasts a long list of local and international celebrity customers who regularly pass through the doors. Framed pictures of many of them adorn the bakery walls!

They still keep to the old, simple traditional recipes, that the locals love. All produce is baked on site by hand and is sourced locally.

Mini Meat, Potato and Onion Pasty

MAKES 24 MINI PASTIES

FILLING

1 kg (2¼ lbs) potatoes, chopped
½ onion, diced
1 teapoon salt
¼ teaspoon white pepper
80 ml (2¾ fl oz) water
150 g (5 oz) minced (ground) beef

PASTRY

150 g (5 oz) lard
500 g (1 lb 2 oz) plain (all-purpose) flour
3 teaspoons salt
240 ml (7¾ fl oz) cold water
1 egg beaten with 1 tablespoon cold water, for the egg wash

FILLING

To make the filling, put the potatoes in a large pan of salted water and bring to the boil. Boil until soft throughout, 10–15 minutes. Meanwhile, put the onions, salt, pepper and water into a medium pan over a high heat and bring to the boil. Add the minced beef and stir well. Bring back to the boil and stir frequently and simmer until the meat turns brown. Stir all the filling ingredients together in a bowl. Add a little water to help bring the ingredients together, if needed.

Preheat the oven to 200°C/400°F/Gas mark 6.

PASTRY

To make the pastry, put the lard, flour and salt into a mixing bowl and mix in an electric mixer, or with the tips of your fingers until the mixture resembles breadcrumbs. Add the water slowly until the mixture comes together in a soft pastry.
Divide the pastry into 25 g (1 oz) pieces and allow to rest in the refrigerator for 20 minutes. Roll out each into a circle about 10 cm (4 in) in diameter. Add a tablespoon of filling to the centre of each. Fold half of the pastry over into a half circle and press down the edges. Fold the pressed edge back up slightly, fold in the sides and press down with your fingers. Brush the pasty with egg wash. Bake for 15–20 minutes until golden and cooked through.

North East England and Scotland

Speciality Bakes

Clervaux Artisan Bakery & Café, Darlington, County Durham

. . . .

Bakers
Scott Hayward (Head of Food) and Sam Ainsley
(Head Chef)

Size of Business
3 shops, 22 staff

Type of Bakery
Continental, modern artisan bakery

Clervaux Artisan Bakery & Café is a business with a conscience. Opening its doors, close to Darlington town centre in 2010, the bakery provides therapeutic and vocational training to disadvantaged young people who are enrolled with the Clervaux Trust, a charity that provides essential life skills to those in danger of becoming excluded from society. 'We have seen the impact this enterprise can have on improving quality of life, building self-esteem and helping a young person become more independent and positively contribute to the local community,' says Head of Food Scott Hayward.

'We bake and create very high quality food backed by an ethos of sourcing ingredients from responsible suppliers,' says Head Chef Sam Ainsley. In fact, the Clervaux Artisan Bakery & Cafe won the responsible retailer award at the Darlington Retail Awards in 2012. The company is passionate about using organic and free-range products in their baked goods, incorporating as much of the Trust's farm-grown produce as is feasible. 'The initiative is trying to reconnect people to the land,' says Sam. Scott is passionate about using the best of what's in season as well as locally created, organic produce. The bakery pride themselves on unusual flavour combinations and offering products that are a little bit different from the norm.

Many of the bakers employed by the bakery and café are trained on the job, an experience shared by Scott, who says that he's still learning.

The company is passionate about using organic and free-range products in their baked goods.

Stout, Walnut and Stilton Bread

MAKES 2 LOAVES

10 g (1/3 oz) salt
365 g (13 oz) strong white bread flour, plus extra for dusting
160 g (5½ oz) wholemeal (whole-wheat) bread flour
75 g (2½ oz) Stilton cheese, crumbled
75 g (2½ oz) walnuts, toasted and crushed
5 g (1/6 oz) dried yeast
365 ml (12½ fl oz) stout
10 g (1/3 oz) black treacle (molasses)

Mix the salt and flours together in a large bowl, then add the nuts and cheese. In a separate jug (pitcher), mix the yeast, stout and black treacle together until dissolved. Pour the liquid into the flour and mix together. Work into a dough until all the flour has been incorporated and then knead by hand for 10 minutes on the work surface. Cover and leave to prove in a draught-free place for approximately 1 hour, or until doubled in size.

Divide into 2 equal pieces, each approximately 500 g (1 lb 2 oz). Leave the dough to rest for 10 minutes on the work surface. To begin the final shaping, roll the dough out into a baseball-bat shape tapering to a point at one end, then form into a curl like a snail's shell. Dust with flour, place onto a baking sheet and cover with a large plastic sheet until doubled in size, approximately 45 minutes.

Preheat the oven to 220°C/425°F/Gas mark 7. Bake for 15 minutes, or until golden brown. Allow to cool and enjoy with a glass of real English ale.

Sweethart Coffee & Cake, Consett, County Durham

Bakers
Mark Hart (Owner) and brother Paul Hart

Size of Business
1 shop, 6 staff

Type of Bakery
Coffee shop that sells freshly baked bread
and cakes

Owner Mark followed his father into the building trade, and only turned his hand to baking in order to create a novelty birthday cake for his young son's birthday. So successful was it, that he was soon asked to make cakes for friends and family, and began baking cakes in the evenings. A back operation followed, effectively bringing his building career to a swift conclusion. Comparing baking to building he says, 'It's just a different type of construction isn't it?'

To finance the opening of the bakery Mark took out a large loan. 'Most of the equipment we use is secondhand, although I've just splashed out a small fortune on a new spiral dough mixer. I think that most of the ovens and fridges are older than my dad!' he says.

Mark is a self-taught baker. 'Some of my recipes come from family, some are published recipes that I've tweaked and others come from a need to use up leftovers,' he says. At the start of the week Mark makes four types of 'standard' loaf, and as the week goes on, the breads he creates take on a more exotic flavour. He also bakes all the cakes and pastries that the shop sells.

Still in its infancy – the bakery opened in June 2012 – the business is now flourishing, with a loyal customer base. Mark's brother helps out two days a week and he has been able to take on an apprentice. Mark takes plenty of pride in his success.

Comparing baking to building Mark says, 'It's just a different type of construction isn't it?'

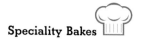

Egg Custard tart

MAKES 1 TART

PASTRY
150 g (6 oz) plain (all-purpose) flour, plus extra for dusting
75 g (2½ oz) butter
70 g (2¼ oz) caster (superfine) sugar
1 small egg
Cold water

FILLING
525 ml (18 fl oz) whipping cream
150 g (5 oz) or approximately 8 egg yolks
85 g (3 oz) caster (superfine) sugar
Nutmeg, grated (ground)

Preheat the oven to 170°C/340°F/Gas mark 3½.

PASTRY
In a food processor, blitz the flour and butter together until it resembles fine breadcrumbs. Stir the sugar through. Mix in as much of the whole egg and sufficient cold water as needed to form a dough – you may not need it all. Knead a little to combine. Roll out the pastry on a lightly floured surface until it's large enough to fit the base and sides of a 23 cm (9 in) diameter flan case. Scrunch up some baking paper, then unwrap it. Place on the pastry, then fill with baking beans. Blind bake for about 15 minutes, or until golden. Reduce the oven temperature to 110°C/225°F/Gas mark ¼.

FILLING
Meanwhile, mix all the filling ingredients together, except for the nutmeg, in a large bowl. Leaving the baked flan case in the oven, remove the paper and baking beans and pour the filling into the case. Liberally sprinkle the surface with nutmeg, then bake for 40–50 minutes. The tart is baked when there is a jelly-like wobble in the centre. Leave to cool and serve cold.

Original Bakehouse, Newcastle-upon-Tyne

Bakers
Simon and Fred Wake

Type of Business
Artisan bakery and coffee shop

Size of Business
1 shop, 16 staff

Simon became a full-time baker in 1999, turning his hand to a trade that is in his blood. Both his parents are bakers and successfully ran a wholesale bakery business, which employed 90 staff at its peak. Today, Simon has one shop that incorporates a bakery. It's still a family-run affair with his parents, cousins and aunts all helping out.

Simon's philosophy is to return to traditional methods of baking. He says, 'We still stick to my founding philosophy and make everything by hand using my Dad's recipes, which were acquired during a lifetime of baking, as well as those passed down the generations… A lot of independent high street bakers have gone now and we are trying to give that traditional taste that everyone wants.' Simon is a perfectionist and takes great pride in the products he makes. He says, 'It's about trying to cut out the need for additives. We want to take baking back to how it used to be.'

Simon makes all the ferments, the bread and rolls for the shop. 'Our customers love local products such as the oven-bottom stottie. However, I'm constantly trialling products and at the weekends our sourdough, Italian ciabatta, six-seed multigrain bread and carrot cake are some of the shop's biggest sellers,' he says.

'We want to take baking back to how it used to be.'

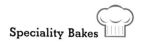

Oven-Bottom Stottie

MAKES 6 LARGE OR 15 SMALL

1 kg (2¼ lb) strong white bread flour, plus extra for dusting
20 g (¾ oz) salt
10 g (⅓ oz) milk powder
10 g (⅓ oz) sugar
30 ml (generous 1 fl oz) sunflower oil

30 g (1 oz) live yeast
650 ml (1 pint and 2 fl oz) water

Note: If using dried yeast, dissolve 12 g (½ oz) of dried yeast in 100 ml (3½ fl oz) of the water and set aside for 10 minutes.

Sift the flour into a large bowl, add the salt, milk powder, sugar, oil, yeast and 500 ml (17 fl oz) of the water. Mix together. As the mix starts to form a dough add the rest of the water and mix until a smooth silky dough is achieved. Cover with cling film (plastic wrap) or a damp cloth and et aside to rest for 30 minutes.

Divide the dough into 120 g (4 oz) balls for small oven-bottom stotties and 300 g (10½ oz) balls for large oven-bottom stotties. Leave to prove at room temperature for 30–45 minutes, or until the dough has doubled in size. On a lightly floured surface, gently roll out the dough balls into flat discs about 0.5 cm (¼ in) thick and 12 cm (5 in) in diameter for the small breads and 24 cm (9½ in) for the large. Be careful not to knock all of the air bubbles out of the dough at this stage. Place on a flat surface. Cover and leave to stand for 30–40 minutes, or until the dough has doubled in height. Preheat the oven to 240°C/475°F/ Gas mark 9. Place the baking sheets in the oven to warm.

Use the handle end of a knife to make a hole in the centre of each disc to allow the air to escape while baking. Slide the bread onto the pre-heated baking sheet. Bake for approximately 4 minutes, or until the underside is starting to colour and the centre has risen equally. Turn the bread over and bake for another 4 minutes. The stottie is ready when the top has a deep red colour with a white centre and a white ring around the edge. Turn the bread over so that the original bread underside is back on the bottom. Place on a wire rack and allow to cool.

The Angel's Share, Richmond, North Yorkshire

Bakers
Alex Franks (Owner) and Di Dinsdale (Baker)

Type of Bakery
Artisan bakery

Size of Business
1 shop, 2 staff

'The angel's share' is a term synonymous with whisky-making. During the distillation process a percentage of the liquid volume is lost; this lost percentage is known as the angel's share. The phrase resonated with Alex, who joked with her father that she would name her first restaurant after it.

Despite a passion for food, Alex went to Newcastle University to study languages and from there took a fast-track graduate scheme into banking. After just two years, Alex had the chance to appear on the popular MasterChef programme and quickly reassessed her career options. Then, after sampling different types of work in the food industry, she opened a deli in Darlington. Five years ago, she opened the bakery in the newly renovated Richmond station, in response to a desire to supply high-quality local bread.

Alex has two permanent staff, Di and Alice. Alice makes the traybakes, pastry and the orders. Di makes the bread, shortbreads, biscuits and amaretti, while Alex makes pastry, cakes, tarts and the daily savouries, with the help of her Mum, Gill. Lots of the bakery's products are adapted from family recipes, 'some from my Grandma who was a baker in her early years… some from travels, books, and reworked ideas,' Alex says. The bread flavours often change, 'the types of breads we make each day are very mood driven'. Their Lancer loaf is named after the local regiment, and other loaves are named after nearby villages. The bakery uses a mix of flours in their products, some of which are local. The bakery layout is wide open so that customers can see Alex and her team making the bread and cakes in front of them. 'People are able to interact with us while we are busy producing, so they know that whatever they are buying could not be fresher,' says Alex.

'In the bakery we have a spiral and a planetary mixer and a prover/retarder to help make life easier, but all the pastry and biscuits are rolled by hand and we hand cut and shape the bread. We're fairly low tech', she says. Popular regional bakes include Yorkshire curd tarts and fat rascals.

Alice makes the traybakes, pastry and the orders. Di makes the bread, shortbreads, biscuits and amaretti, while Alex and Gill make pastry, cakes, tarts and the daily savouries.

Cumberland Ham, Apple and Sage Pie

MAKES 1 LARGE PIE AND SERVES 12

PASTRY

300 g (10½ oz) plain (all-purpose) flour, plus extra for dusting
175 g (6 oz) butter
30 g (1 oz) vegetable fat
Salt and pepper
1 egg yolk
300 g (10½ oz) ready-made puff pastry
1 egg, lightly beaten

FILLING

1 kg (2¼ lb) good quality pork sausagemeat
250 g (9 oz) ham, cubed
1 leek, finely chopped
1 egg
2 eating apples, peeled and grated (shredded)
Dried sage, to taste
Pepper
Freshly grated nutmeg

Preheat the oven to 200°C/400°F/Gas mark 6.

PASTRY

To make the pastry, put the flour in a food processor with the cold butter and process lightly until the mixture resembles breadcrumbs. Add the vegetable fat and process again, very gently. Empty the pastry mix into a large bowl, and season with salt and pepper. In a jug, mix the egg yolk with 200 ml (7 fl oz) of water, pour into the pastry mix and bind together with a fork until it forms a ball. Knead until the dough just comes together. Roll out the pastry on a lightly floured surface and use to line a 30 cm (12 in) diameter loose-base flan case. Line with aluminium foil and weigh down with baking beans. Bake blind in the hot oven for approximately 18 minutes.

FILLING

Meanwhile, to make the filling, put the sausagemeat into a large bowl. Add the ham, leek, egg, apples, sage, pepper and a generous pinch of nutmeg. Stir everything together until combined. Pour into the baked pastry case until level with the top of the crust.

On a lightly floured surface, roll out the puff pastry until it is 4 mm (⅛ in) thick. Use the beaten egg to moisten the edge of the baked pastry case, roll the puff pastry over the top of the flan filling and crimp all around the edges. Score a pattern on the top. Glaze with the egg and bake for about 1 hour.

Jeanette's Cakery, Saltaire, West Yorkshire

Bakers
Jeanette Blackburn (Owner)

Type of Bakery
Pâtisserie serving soups, sandwiches, coffee, afternoon tea and a wide selection of American-inspired goodies

Size of Business
1 shop, 7 staff

Set in one of the original buildings at the World Heritage site of Saltaire, the model village surrounding the textile mill built by industrialist Sir Titus Salt in 1851, Jeanette's Cakery is a cosy time capsule that harks back to the 1940s and '50s.

All seven employees dress the part in period outfits made by Jeanette's mum and each has their name embroidered onto their apron. Every detail is considered and everyone has their hair rolled daily! 'The majority of our staff sing,' says Jeanette. 'We hold special evenings for our live singing events, though we have been known to spontaneously burst into song!' Jeanette knows her customers well, 'I think people enjoy reminiscing about other eras – particularly wartime. Added to that, the coffee we serve is great and the customers love the outfits. We just sometimes struggle to fit everyone in – bookings are essential at weekends!'

Jeanette lived in America for two years, so she uses recipes inspired by her time there. 'I create my own cheesecakes, which are a result of my own experimentation. I like to add my own twist.' She says her baking style is quite traditional. Jeanette makes everything using a Kitchenaid mixer in 'the world's smallest kitchen'. A chef by training, Jeanette says her baking style is 'quite traditional'. The pâtisserie was awarded the 2012 National Beverage Standards Awards – 4 cups accreditation.

Jeanette lived in America for two years, so she uses recipes inspired by her time there.

Coffee and Walnut Cake

MAKES 1 LARGE CAKE

SPONGE

340 g (11¾ oz) margarine, plus extra for greasing

340 g (11¾ oz) caster (superfine) sugar

6 eggs

340 g (11¾ oz) self-raising (self-rising) flour

75–90 ml (2½–3 fl oz) good-quality espresso, cooled

120 g (4 oz) walnuts, chopped

FROSTING AND FILLING

120 g (4 oz) butter

120 g (4 oz) margarine

460 g (1 lb) icing (confectioners') sugar

25 ml (1 fl oz) good-quality espresso, cooled

Handful of walnuts, crushed, for decoration

Preheat the oven to 170°C/310°F/Gas mark 3½. Grease and line two round cake tins (pans) each 23 cm (9 in) diameter.

SPONGE

To make the cake, cream the margarine and sugar in a large bowl until pale. Beat in the eggs and the flour. Add the coffee and walnuts and mix until well combined. Divide the batter between the prepared cake tins. Bake for 25–30 minutes, or until risen and golden and a skewer, when inserted into the centre, comes out clean. Leave to set in the tin for a few minutes before turning out on to a wire rack to go cold.

FROSTING AND FILLING

To make the frosting, beat the butter, margarine and icing sugar together in a large bowl until light and fluffy. Stir in the espresso. Place one sponge on a serving plate, top with half the frosting and spread evenly to the edges. Add the second cake sponge, then spread the rest of the frosting on top. Scatter crushed walnuts on top, for decoration.

The Sunflower Bakery, Dore, Sheffield

Bakers
Tanya and Ron Shrimpton

Size of Business
1 shop, 4 staff

Type of Bakery
Artisan bread bakery with small selection of cakes

The Sunflower Bakery literally began as a cottage industry back in September 2011. Tanya, the baker, would make four different types of bread and sell them at WI country markets. She quickly realised the demand for homemade bread saying, 'customers would grab the loaves as if it were treasure'. The shop opened in December 2012, a collaboration between herself and husband Ron, who is the front of house sales person.

Tanya has more than 30 years of baking experience, having studied bakery and confectionery production at university in Kiev, before working for industrial bakeries in her homeland. With a strong understanding of the science behind the process, she loves to experiment with different flours, ingredients and techniques, and often takes requests from local customers. Tanya incorporates traditional Russian and Eastern European recipes into her bakes, working from memory to recreate her products and continues to develop a range of bread that will satisfy traditional English tastes.

> With a strong understanding of the science behind the process, Tanya loves to experiment with different flours.

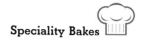

Sourdough Dark Rye Bread 'Borodinski'

MAKES 1 LOAF

Sunflower oil, for greasing
265 g (9½ oz) wholemeal (whole-wheat) rye flour
250 g (9 oz) rye sourdough starter (*see introduction*)
25 g (¾ oz) malted rye flour
¾ teaspoons coriander seeds, ground

¾ teaspoons caraway seeds, ground
200 ml (7 fl oz) water
20 g (¾ oz) golden (light corn) syrup
150 g (5 oz) strong white bread flour
¼ teaspoon dried yeast
1½ teaspoons salt
Whole coriander seeds, for decoration

Grease one x 900 g (2 lb) loaf tin (pan) with oil.

In a large bowl, mix together 225 g (8 oz) of the wholemeal rye flour, the sourdough starter and 100–150 ml (3½–5 fl oz) tepid (27–29°C/80–84°F) water to make a very thick paste. Leave to ferment for 3½–4 hours.

Meanwhile, mix together the rye malt flour, remaining wholemeal rye flour, ground coriander and caraway seeds. Add sufficient boiling water to make a thick paste, cover and leave to cool.

Dissolve the golden syrup in 50 ml (2 fl oz) of warm water in a jug.

Tip the second flour mixture into the first, add the strong bread flour, dried yeast, salt, and golden syrup and water mixture and mix until well combined as a very thick paste. Leave the dough to ferment for 30–60 minutes depending on the temperature of the dough, which should be about 27–29°C/80–84°F). Use a plastic scraper, dipped in water to divide the dough into four, shape and place each into a prepared loaf tin. Smooth the surface of each, mist with water and top with coriander seeds. Leave to rise for 45–60 minutes.

Preheat the oven to 220°C/425°F/Gas mark 7. Bake the loaves for approximately 30 minutes, or until dark brown, adding a tray of water to the base of the oven to create steam while the bread is baking.

Lawton's Pies, Leek, Staffordshire

. . . .

Owners
Steve and Alison Ball, husband and wife

Size of Business
2 shops, 7 staff

Type of Bakery
Traditional meat pies, bread and cakes

Lawton's Pies opened for business almost 90 years ago in the heart of the town centre, albeit trading as Winkles Bakery, and the recipes that served the generations in the opening decades of the twentieth century are still made and served in the shop today, as popular now as they ever were. Not surprisingly the name and product are well established in Leek and the surrounding area. Steve and Alison, the business owners, are both self-taught bakers who took on the business 13 years ago. They take pride in sourcing local ingredients for use in their products and all items sold within the bakery are created on site. In fact, much of it is made using machinery that has served the bakery well for more than 50 years. The company prides itself on hand-making items, with all cakes and bread prepared on 'the bench'. The duo believe their simple approach to baking is successful. The bakery is their life; a lifestyle choice that has served them well. The business is thriving and continues to go from strength to strength each year. Customers are known to queue out of the door in order to purchase one of their 'famous' pies — the company sells 2000 of these per week. Though all the recipes were purchased with the business, new ideas are introduced, such as the chicken and vegetable pie, a delicious consequence of recipe trial and error.

The company prides itself on hand-making items, with all cakes and bread prepared on 'the bench'.

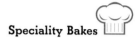

Bread Pudding

MAKES 1

250 g (9 oz) white bread (stale is best)
50 g (1¾ oz) currants and sultanas (golden raisins)
Pinch of mixed (apple pie) spice
50 g (1¾ oz) demerara (raw) sugar

1 egg
300 ml (½ pint) milk
65 g (2¼ oz) butter, plus extra for greasing
65 g (2¼ oz) marmalade
Vanilla extract, to taste

Grease a 1 litre (1 pint) rectangular baking dish with butter. Tear up the bread into small pieces into a large mixing bowl. Add the dried fruit, mixed spice and most of the sugar (save some for sprinkling on the top). In another bowl, beat the egg with the milk. Pour the milk mixture over the bread and mix together.

Melt the butter with the marmalade in a small pan over medium heat, and stir to combine. Add the vanilla, stir through then pour over the bread mixture. Stir and let stand for 10 minutes.

Meanwhile, preheat the oven to 190°C/375°F/Gas mark 5. Pour the mixture into the prepared baking dish, top with sugar and bake for 30–40 minutes, or until golden.

Spondon Bakery, Spondon, Derbyshire

Bakers
Vagelis Giakalis (Owner), Jordan (Apprentice)

Size of Business
1 shop, 4 staff

Type of Bakery
Traditional with a Greek twist

A third-generation baker, Vagelis Giakalis learnt his trade from his father and grandfather in his native Greece. After marrying a Brit, he and his family moved to the UK with the intention of becoming self-sufficient. With their surplus stock the couple began to sell bakery products, jams and chutneys at local fairs and markets, culminating in the bakery opening in autumn 2012.

We have our own smallholding that houses a breeding herd of around 40 goats and rare breed Portland sheep, and around 150 rare breed chickens. We follow the process through from start to finish. That means that we have a breeding programme, deliver the kids, rear them, take them to slaughter, then use the meat in our pies. We are involved in the process from start to finish.

Ninety-nine percent of the products in our shop are made by us, and all the ingredients that make up those products are locally sourced or from the allotment. We concentrate on seasonal fruit and vegetables. Our shop is about local, homemade produce; what we grow, breed, make and bake. We have a low carbon footprint. Customers can buy our

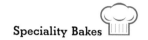

bread, and spread it with our conserves, which are made from the fruit we have picked from our allotment, or the hedgerows in our smallholding,' says Vagelis.

Vagelis bakes everything by hand on site with the help of his wife and two apprentices. 'We are a small independent family village bakery, making bread, pies, cakes, biscuits, and also our own brand of jam, marmalades, chutneys and cordials,' he says. 'A village bakery needs to meet the needs of the locals and those that travel into it. We want to keep the village centre alive. Every village shop that closes is a loss to the community. Ditch the car, save on parking and fuel, and use your local shops!'

We combine Greek and English dishes in our shop, and the Greek recipes that we use have been passed through the generations. Others are successful experiments or influenced by existing dishes.

'We are a small independent family village bakery, making bread, pies, cakes, biscuits, and also our own brand of jam, marmalades, chutneys and cordials.'

Chorizo and Caramelised Onion Loaf

MAKES 4 LOAVES

200 g (7 oz) red onion, sliced
200 g (7 oz) brown sugar
2 oz (60 g) butter
200 g (7 oz) chorizo, finely chopped
1 kg (2¼ lbs) plain (all-purpose) flour, plus extra for dusting
30 g (1 oz) yeast

500 ml (17 fl oz) lukewarm water
1 teaspoon salt
1 teaspoon sugar
1 tablespoon butter

Fry the sliced red onions and brown sugar with a little butter in a pan for about 1 hour, over a very low heat, until caramelised and then set aside. Fry the chorizo in a frying pan over medium heat for 5 minutes, or until cooked and then set aside.

To make the bread dough, combine the flour, yeast, warm water, salt, sugar and butter in a large bowl and mix to bring the ingredients together. Turn out onto a lightly floured surface and knead for 10–20 minutes, or until it is elastic. Add the cooked onion and chorizo to the dough, mix gently to incorporate and leave to prove for 10 minutes in a covered bowl. Divide the dough into 200 g (7 oz) portions and put in the tins (pans). Leave the loaves to prove for 1 hour, until they have doubled in size.

Preheat the oven to 200°C/400°F/Gas mark 6. Bake for approximately 30 minutes. Test by removing the bread from the tin and tapping the base of each loaf; the sound should be hollow and the bread light.

The Pudding Room, Ashbourne, Derbyshire

Bakers
Angie Cooper (Owner) and Mary (Assistant)

Type of Bakery
Traditional puddings, pastries and cakes

Size of Business
1 shop, 2 staff

Bakery owner Angie is self-taught and has been baking puddings ever since she can remember. A nurse by training, she started out making puddings for her colleagues and when demand soared she left her job to start up her own business. Back in 2001 Angie's cottage industry began in her own kitchen. Four years later she expanded into the garage and then into a converted stable block with its own shop.

Angie makes and sells simple, traditional dishes and is extremely passionate about incorporating local products into her recipes. She's helped by Mary whose background is in confectionery.

Based just outside the Peak District, Angie thrives by providing locals and tourists with her pudding treats. She also attends farmers markets at Wirksworth, Belper and Bakewell where her lemon meringue pie, crunchy apple tart and Victoria sponges go down a treat. Angie also takes part in local shows during the summer – Derbyshire County Show, Ashover Show, Ashbourne Show and Derbyshire Day.

Angie's cottage industry began in her own kitchen. Four years later she expanded into the garage.

Lemon Meringue Pie

MAKES 1

PASTRY
240 g (8¾ oz) plain (all-purpose) flour, plus extra for dusting
60 g (2 oz) lard
60 g (2 oz) vegetable margarine
Water, to bind

LEMON FILLING
150 g (5 oz) sugar
4 egg yolks
2 lemons, zest and juice
300 ml (½ pint) water
60 g (2 oz) cornflour (corn starch) mixed with a little water to
    make a paste

MERINGUE
4 egg whites
240 g (8¾ oz) sugar

PASTRY
To make the pastry, put the flour, lard and margarine in a bowl or electric mixer and rub in, or process, until the mixture resembles breadcrumbs. Add just enough water to bind the breadcrumbs together. Tip out onto a lightly floured work surface and knead lightly until it comes together in a ball.

Roll out the dough to line a 20 cm (8 in) loose-base flan tin. Refrigerate to rest for 10 minutes. Meanwhile preheat the oven to 190°C/375°F/Gas mark 5. Line the pastry in the tin with baking paper and fill with baking beans or weights. Bake blind for 10 minutes, then remove the paper and baking beans and bake for another 5 minutes. Leave to cool. Lower the oven temperature to 170°C/310°F/Gas mark 3½.

LEMON FILLING
To make the filling, put the sugar, egg yolks, lemon zest and juice and water in a saucepan. Place over a medium heat and bring to a rolling boil for 5–10 minutes. Remove from the heat. Stir the cornflour paste into the hot lemon mix. Allow to thicken. Pour into the baked pastry case.

MERINGUE
In a bowl, beat the egg whites using an electric mixer and whisk, until thick peaks form. Leave the mixer turned on and add the sugar gradually. Keep mixing until the egg whites are thick and glossy. Pour on top of the lemon filling. Bake for 20 minutes, or until the meringue is hard to touch.

Bakery Andante, Edinburgh

Bakers
Jon (Owner) and Steffen (Master Baker)

Type of Bakery
Artisan bread bakery

Size of Business
1 bakery, 4 bakers

Bakery Andante is Edinburgh's artisan bakery with a penchant for making sourdough breads. In fact, the company offers one of the largest ranges in the local area. Flavoured breads, brownies, cakes, traybakes and croissants make up the complement of baked goods that this thriving bakery has on offer. Jon says, 'We are one of the few bakeries that make our own croissants. I love the fact that they're made using local milk and butter.'

Every product is made from scratch using only natural ingredients. 'By making as much as we can on the premises we can control all elements. We can use local suppliers and ingredients and as a result we have a product line with plenty of flavour and texture,' he says.

Andante is a musical expression meaning 'at a slower pace', which sums up this bakery's approach. Steffen says, 'Our main focus is to provide very high quality fresh bread to our customers. Many of our breads aren't out of the oven until after 8 am. A customer that comes in at 10 am can still get a warm loaf and know that it's fresh.'

Baking was Jon's hobby for years, but when he was made redundant in November 2010 he decided that he didn't want to return to an office job so took the plunge and opened Bakery Andante. In fact, he still thinks of himself as a 'hobbyist' rather than a professional baker. 'I am mainly self-taught with a lot of on-the-job training and trial and error learning. When I was setting up I was lucky to receive a lot of help and support. I took a short course on baking for profit run by the organisation Bread Matters. Additionally, Scottish Bakers, the body that represents bakers in Scotland, gave me fantastic support, and other bakers allowed me to spend time with them to see how the professionals did it, which was very generous of them, and a huge learning experience.' He adds, 'It's been hard work establishing the business; however, the great feedback from our fantastic customers makes it all worthwhile.'

'We are one of the few bakeries that make our own croissants. I love the fact that they're made using local milk and butter.'

Covenanters Bread

● ●

MAKES 1 X 2 KG (4½ LB) LOAF

250 g (9 oz) sourdough starter, refreshed and lively (*see*
   Before You Begin)
290 g (10¼ oz) strong white bread flour
950 g (2 lb 2 oz) dark flour (see tip)
760 ml (1¼ pints) warm water
24 g (1 oz) salt

In an electric mixer, or by hand, mix the sour starter, flours and water for 4 minutes at a slow speed or until all the flour is combined. Cover and allow to rest for 20–40 minutes. Add the salt and mix on a slow speed, or gently knead for 4 minutes until the salt is combined and the dough is just starting to form. Cover (use a sealed bucket, damp dish towel, lightly oiled plastic or cling film (plastic wrap) and set aside for 2 hours, in a warm place.

Carefully empty the dough out onto a lightly floured work surface and pull a corner of the dough over to the centre. Repeat for each 'corner'. Cover and set aside for 30 minutes.

Gently turn and fold (repeating as above). Cover and set aside for another 30 minutes.

The dough should now be active, with some large bubbles appearing in the dough. Shape into a tight ball (trying to keep as much air in the dough as possible). Place into a proofing basket, or use a large mixing bowl lined with a floured dish towel, cover and leave to rise for 1 hour.

Preheat the oven to 230°C/450°F/Gas mark 8 and add a baking sheet to the oven to warm. Bake the bread on the baking sheet for 55 minutes. When it is ready, it should have a dense crust and should sound hollow when tapped on the base.

Tip: Dark flour is a specific type of flour, which can be purchased from Shipton Mill (Swiss Dark) or you could use 50:50 wholemeal (whole-wheat) and white, but put the wholemeal though a food processor to make the bran finer.

Blair Atholl Watermill & Tearoom, Perthshire

Bakers
Rami (Owner) and Stuart (Baker)

Type of Bakery
Artisan bakery

Size of Business
1 bakery and 10 staff (at the height of the season)

Bakery owner Rami is originally from Israel. He met his wife Kirsty in Australia and the two returned to his homeland to become farmers. When they received the news that Kirsty's parents wanted to sell the watermill, the two decided to move to Scotland to carry on running it. Rami says, 'We sold our cows back in Israel and gave up the lease on our land, so there's no going back'.

The business is based within a watermill, which has just celebrated its 400th anniversary and the bakery is based in what was once the stables for the coal horses back in the 1800s. 'The watermill is key equipment for us. It's dependent on the weather, but that doesn't seem to be an issue in Scotland! We are very proud to have a working mill'. It's the only operational mill left in Perthshire and exclusively it grinds the bakery's own oats and wheat.

The bakery keeps its equipment simple, which allows the company to create bread as it has been produced for thousands of years. Rami learnt to bake from Kirsty's mother Mary, and over the years he has expanded the range produced at the watermill. He now also specialises in bread making and running bread-making courses.

Fellow baker Stuart specialises in baking cakes. Despite being only 19, Rami describes Stuart as being very hard working and passionate about food. Rami says, 'we are very lucky with our staff. Some have been with us since their teens. We have a fantastic team of loyal employees.'

'Our motto and ethos is that we produce what we believe in and enjoy to eat for ourselves. Tasty wholesome food without anything that shouldn't be there. Our basic philosophy is to keep it simple, choose good ingredients and check their source of origin. Some of the recipes, though, are family ones, such as Kirsty's carrot cake, which has proved to be very popular. We try to use local produce in our recipes and choose not to use additives or preservatives. Real bread shouldn't last', says Rami.

'Our motto and ethos is that we produce what we believe in and enjoy to eat for ourselves. Tasty wholesome food without anything that shouldn't be there.'

Bagels

MAKES 10–14

250 g (9 oz) strong white bread flour
150 g (5 oz) wholemeal (whole-wheat) flour
100 g (3½ oz) malted wheat flour
2 eggs (one for egg wash)
15 g (½ oz) salt, plus 1 teaspoon, for the boiling mix
2 teaspoons sugar
25 ml (1 fl oz) sunflower oil
10 g (1/3 oz) yeast (one sachet of dry yeast)

40 g (1¼ oz) black treacle (molasses), plus 20 g (¾ oz), for the boiling mix
280–320 ml (9–11 fl oz) water, for the dough mix
1 egg white mixed with 1 tablespoon of cold water, for glazing
Poppy seeds, sunflower seeds or sesame seeds, to garnish

Mix all of the ingredients together in a large bowl, except for the seeds for garnishing. Add a little more water or flour, if needed, to make a soft, but not sticky, dough. Knead for 10 minutes or until the dough becomes smooth and silky. Cover and set aside to prove for a couple of hours until the dough has doubled in size. Divide the dough into 70–100 g (2½–3½ oz) pieces – there should be around 12. Add your choice of flavours (see below). Shape the dough pieces into rolls, leave to rest for 5–10 minutes, covering with a damp dish towel if the environment is warm.

Bring 2 litres (3½ pints) of water to a boil in a large saucepan, add the extra teaspoon of salt and the extra treacle. Meanwhile, preheat the oven to the hottest setting. Put your finger through the centre of the bread roll and spin around your finger to create a hole. Put 4 bagels in the pan and boil each side for no more than 30 seconds, remove with a slotted spoon, drain and arrange on a baking tray. Repeat until all the bagels are shaped and boiled.

Brush the bagels with the egg white and water mix. Scatter with poppy seeds, sunflower seeds or sesame seeds. Bake for 8–12 minutes, or until golden on top. Set aside to cool on a wire rack.

BAGEL FLAVOURS

Cinnamon bagels: For every 100 g (3½ oz) of dough add 5 g (1 teaspoon) cinnamon, 20 g (¾ oz) sultanas (golden raisins) and raisins, presoaked in a little water. Cinnamon bagels should be toasted before eating to bring out the cinnamon flavour.
Oatmeal and onion: Add finely chopped fried onion and oatmeal (pinhead/steel cut oats can be fried with the onion, or use medium oats, stoneground) in the proportion of 1 part oats and onions to 5 parts dough.

Garvald Bakery, Edinburgh

Bakers
Alistair Baines and Louise Muir

Size of Business
3 staff (plus up to 12 bakers

Type of Bakery
Artisan breads produced by adults with learning
disabilities

Unusually Garvald Bakery has no shop front. Its customers phone to reserve their loaves and then call by to collect it. Al manages the bakery, which provides a safe and inclusive environment for adults with learning disabilities, and involves them in every aspect of baking. Al says, 'I originally worked in catering and have run coffee shops in the past, but I was bored and wanted to give something back to my community, so I began working at Garvald. I've lost track of how long I've been here – nine, maybe ten years.'

The bakery, which has been operational for more than 40 years, specialises in organic, artisan breads which are made by two bakers, with up to 12 adults with learning disabilities working alongside. Its recipes are tried-and-tested, usually either donated by friends, gathered from books, or passed on by fellow bread enthusiasts. The bakery also sells wholesale to more than a dozen local, independent stores.

The bakery holds the distinction of being certified by the Organic Food Federation.

The bakery provides a safe and inclusive environment for adults with learning disabilities and involves them in every aspect of baking.

Sourdough

· ·

MAKES 1 LOAF

10 g (¹/₃ oz) wholemeal (whole-wheat) sourdough starter (*see Before You Begin*)

35 g (1¼ oz) wholemeal (whole-wheat) flour

35 ml (scant 2 tablespoons) warm water

175 g (6 oz) wholemeal (whole-wheat) flour

35 g (1¼ oz) white sourdough starter (see Before You Begin)

130 ml (generous 4 fl oz) cold water

350 g (12 oz) strong white bread flour

10 g (¹/₃ oz) salt

In a large bowl, combine the wholemeal sourdough starter, wholemeal flour and warm water to make a wet paste-like dough and set aside, covered with a wet cloth, for at least 4 hours.

Add the next batch of wholemeal flour, the sourdough starter and the cold water to the first mix and mix thoroughly with a wooden spoon, or in mixer with a dough attachment. Cover and set aside, preferably overnight.

Add the strong white bread flour and the salt to the mixture with approximately 350 ml (12 fl oz) of warm water to make a soft dough. Mix for 10 minutes. Set aside covered with a wet cloth for 4 hours.

Shape the loaf or put in a loaf tin (pan) and leave to prove for at least 2 hours. Preheat the oven to 200°C/400°F/Gas mark 6) and put in a baking sheet to heat up. Turn out the bread onto the pre-heated baking sheet, slash the top along the centre then bake for 30–40 minutes.

Wales and the Midlands

Becws Mefus, Isle of Anglesey

· ·

Owner/Baker
Benjamin Lee (Owner) and Patricia Williams (Baker)

Type of Bakery
Small craft bakery producing award-winning celebration cakes

Size of Business
2 shops, 6 staff

Quality and attention to detail are bakery owner Benjamin Lee's guiding principles. Benjamin started baking at 15years of age, and purchased the bakery 5 years ago from a retired couple in order to pursue his passion for creating quality cakes, bread and fine chocolate work.

Benjamin's wife, Olwen, joined the business three years ago after leaving her job as a PA to a principal at a college, and now works as a partner. Since the company has become established, Benjamin has opened a second shop specialising in celebration cakes and hand-made chocolates.

His bakery has won awards for its cakes and bread. Benjamin says, 'People flock in for the traditional bara brith, a huge range of specialist breads and Victoria sponges on a daily basis'. Benjamin likes to make traditional Welsh recipes but is also very innovative, saying he believes the people of north Wales and Anglesey are ready for new culinary experiences. The bakery has a viewing window, through which customers can watch the bakers at work. Benjamin won the award for Regional Best Wedding Cake Maker in Wales in 2011 and again in 2013.

'People flock in for the traditional bara brith, Welsh cakes and Victoria sponges on a daily basis'.

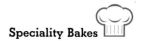
Bara Brith

. . . .

MAKES 3

STAGE 1
225 g (8 oz) butter, plus extra for greasing
750 g (1 lb 11 oz) soft brown sugar
225 g (8 oz) sultanas
1 teaspoon bicarbonate of soda (baking soda)
150 ml (¼ pint) water

STAGE 2
340 g (11¾ oz) plain (all-purpose) flour
1 teaspoon mixed (apple pie) spice
2 eggs

STAGE 1
Place all the stage 1 ingredients into a heavy pan and set over medium heat. Stir regularly and bring to the boil. Once boiling, remove from the heat and allow to go completely cold; allow several hours.

Preheat the oven to 180°C/350°F/Gas mark 4. Grease and line 3 small loaf tins (pans).

STAGE 2
Pour the cold cake batter into an electric mixer and add the stage 2 ingredients. Beat on low speed for 1 minute, then medium speed for 2–3 minutes, until glossy and smooth. Divide the batter between the prepared tins and bake for 60 minutes. Leave to set in the tins for a few minutes before turning out onto a wire rack to go cold.

St Mary's Bakery, Brecon

Owner
Ashley Moses (Owner) and Mikey

Type of Bakery
Traditional Welsh bakery

Size of Business
2 shops, 24 staff

Born and bred in Brecon, head baker Ashley is proud of his Welsh roots and has a passion for Welsh produce.

He considers it his task to make the bread while Mikey, his Hungarian baker, who is a trained confectioner, makes all of the cakes. Together they have been baking for 40 years and can turn their hands to all types of baking.

The bakery has attracted a lot of local media attention recently but for all the wrong reasons, since it caught fire last year due to an electrical fault in a flat above. They subsequently had to rebuild the bakery. Fortunately once the bakery reopened, the continued support from the local community kept them in business.

The two bake 90 percent of their produce on site and the majority of the ingredients they use are sourced locally. All their bread is baked in their Welsh wood-burning oven and Ashley collects oak wood from the Brecon Beacons to burn.

St Mary's Bakery has been making and selling baked products for over 110 years.

All their bread is baked in their Welsh wood-burning oven. Ashley collects oak wood from the Brecon Beacons to burn.

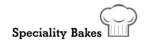

Welsh Black Beef and Ale Pie

MAKES 8–10 PIES

FILLING

1.2 kg (2½ lb) good quality stewing beef, diced
50 ml (2 fl oz) ale
500 g (1 lb 2 oz) onions, diced
340–390 ml (11½–13½ fl oz) water
11.5–22.5 g (⅓–¾ oz) gravy granules

PASTRY

450 g (1 lb) plain (all-purpose) flour, plus extra for dusting
115 g (4 oz) butter, plus extra for greasing
115 g (4 oz) white vegetable fat or shortening
25–50 ml (1–2 fl oz) water
500 g (1 lb 2 oz) puff pastry, for topping
1 egg, lightly beaten, for the egg wash

FILLING

To make the filling put the beef and ale in a cooking pot and refrigerate for 24 hours.

Preheat the oven to 180°C/350°F/Gas mark 4.

Mix the onions into the beef and ale mix and stir in 140–190 ml (4½– 6½ fl oz) water. Bake for 3–4 hours. Remove the casserole from the oven and drain the juice into a large pan. To make the gravy, pour the gravy granules into a bowl, add the rest of the cold water, mix to a smooth paste, then add the liquid to the meat juices in the pan. Heat over a medium heat and simmer for 10 minutes. Add the beef and onion mix, stir, then leave to cool.

PASTRY

To make the pastry, place the flour, butter and shortening into the bowl of an electric mixer and blend to a fine crumb. Add the water gradually until it just comes together. Tip out onto a lightly floured surface, knead slightly, then roll out to 6 mm (¼ in) thick.

Preheat the oven to 230°C/450°F/Gas mark 8. Lightly grease 8–9 pie dishes each 10 cm (4 in) in diameter and 3–4 cm (1¼–1½ in) deep. Fill the pie case with the pie filling.

On a lightly floured surface, roll out the puff pastry and stamp out rounds to make lids for each pie. Dampen the top edge of the pastry side with water and stick the lids in place. Pinch the edges together. Make a cut in the top of each pastry lid to let the steam escape while cooking. Brush egg wash over the pastry. Bake for 25–30 minutes, until golden.

The Bakers' Table, Talgarth, Powys

Owner
Nicola Willis

Type of Bakery
Artisan bakery and café selling mainly bread,
cakes, pastries, light lunches and pizzas

Size of Business
1 shop, 10 staff

The Bakers' Table is located within a full working mill, which was restored with national lottery funding. The mill supplies flour to the bakery and since it's a tourist attraction, there's plenty of opportunity for them to make and perfect their afternoon tea. All produce is sourced locally and made on site by hand. The duo take pride in the fact that they're one of the only bakeries in Wales that makes croissants by hand and on site. The bakery's speciality is millwheel fougasse. It's made in the shape of a millwheel and is topped with pesto made from local wild garlic and cheese. They're also very proud of their sourdough. 'Every day we bake our favourites, bara havard (white with rye) and bara'r flinwr (seeded wholemeal) and then supplement these with a daily changing range of bakehouse breads including harvest cob (granary style) bara brown and Talgarth Mill brown, which is baked with the lovely flour, ground next door,' they say.

Headed up by Nicola, the hardworking team bake bread, and pastries, cakes, sausage rolls, lunches and daily specials. Local cheese, herbs and fruits are her favoured ingredients for making fabulous tasting products. Some of the herbs are grown in the restored mill's garden, right outside the café door.

Nicola is an experienced baker with quite a repertoire of sweet and savoury dishes. She has worked with food from a young age when she used to help her father in his business, and has won awards for her hand-raised pies. She likes to adapt recipes to make use of local and seasonal ingredients, and has high standards for taste and presentation. She also specialises in making unusual preserves, which add a special twist to the cafe's lunch dishes.

The Bakers' Table is located within a full working mill, which was restored with national lottery funding.

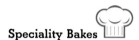

Millwheel Fougasse with Garlic Pesto and Black Mountains Smoked Cheese

MAKES 6 WHEELS

STARTER
5 g (1 teaspoon) fresh yeast
250 g (9 oz) tepid water
50 g (1¾ oz) dark rye flour
200 g (7 oz) strong white bread flour, plus extra for dusting

DOUGH
80 ml (2½ fl oz) water
10 g (¹/₃ oz) salt
250 g (9 oz) strong white bread flour
5 g (1 teaspoon) fresh yeast
Semolina, to dust

PESTO
1 garlic clove, chopped
75 g (2½ oz) walnuts, toasted
50 g (1¾ oz) wild garlic, or spinach. ropcket, parsley or basil
50 g (1¾ oz) smoked cheese
Juice of ½ lemon
Salt and pepper, to taste
50 ml (2 fl oz) olive oil
100 g (3½ oz) Black Mountains smoked cheese

STARTER
To make the starter, in a large bowl, whisk the yeast into the water until dissolved. Add the flours and whisk to a batter. Cover and set aside for 3 hours but not longer than 5 hours in a warm place (27°C/80°F).

DOUGH
Combine the water with the starter and add the dry ingredients. Mix for 5 minutes and then knead on a lightly floured surface for 5 minutes. Place the dough in a clean bowl, cover and leave to prove overnight in the refrigerator. Divide the dough into 6 equal rounds, and rest for 5 minutes. Roll out the dough on a floured surface and cut into it to indicate the spokes of a wheel. Dust with semolina. Set aside.

PESTO
To make the pesto, blitz all the ingredients together in a food processor and thin with olive oil, if necessary, until the consistency drops easily from a spoon. Coat the bread wheels with pesto and scatter the cheese over the top.

Preheat the oven to 240°C/475°F/Gas mark 9. Add baking sheets to the oven to warm. Mist the inside of the hot oven with water. Slide the bread into the oven and onto pre-heated baking sheets. Reduce the oven temperature to 230°C/450°C/Gas mark 8 and bake for 10–12 minutes.

Maison Mayci

Owners
Brothers David and Remi Faveau

Type of Bakery
French bakery and pâtisserie selling breads, cakes
and pastries

Size of Business
2 shops, 1 bakery unit, 10 staff

Maison Mayci is owned by two brothers, David and Remi, who sell traditional French bread, pâtisseries and coffee.

Both attended a prestigious catering school in France, then went on to train at Michelin-starred restaurants. David at restaurant Georges Blanc. Remi at La Pyramide.

The brothers moved to England 10 years ago, continuing their restaurant work. Two years later David opened the bakery and the first shop in Kings Heath, a suburb of Birmingham. Another shop was added in Moseley in 2010. Though the shops have very different identities they sell the same produce. David makes all the baked goods from scratch and Remi runs the shops. David makes traditional, classic, French recipes including some family ones.

'Presentation is the most important element to us,' he says, a fact that is abundantly clear when you look at the precision-made and decorated cakes. The company's bestsellers are croissants and bread.

David uses all traditional, classic, French recipes and some of them are family recipes. 'Presentation is the most important element to us.

Episcopale

• •

MAKES 20

CHARTREUSE MACARON
180 g (6 oz) icing (confectioners') sugar
90 g (3¼ oz) ground almonds (almond meal)
2½ egg whites, at room temperature
Green food colouring (optional)

MACARON FILLING
125 g (4½ oz) caster (superfine) sugar
50 ml (2 fl oz) water
2 eggs
200 g (7 oz) butter, softened
Vanilla, pistachio or chocolate flavouring

SPONGE
4 eggs, separated
125 g (4½ oz) caster (superfine) sugar
125 g (4½ oz) plain (superfine) flour

PASTRY CREAM
2 eggs, separated
65 g (2¼ oz) caster (superfine) sugar
20 g (¾ oz) plain (superfine) flour
20 g (¾ oz) custard powder
250 ml (8 fl oz) milk

CHARTREUSE CREAM
100 ml (3½ fl oz) whipping cream
1 teaspoon agar agar
25 ml (1 fl oz) chartreuse liqueur

CHOCOLATE TRUFFLE
40 g (1¼ oz) glucose
700 ml (1 pint 3½ fl oz) whipping cream
300 g (11 oz) dark (bittersweet) chocolate, melted

GANACHE
300 ml (½ pint) whipping cream
40 g (1¼ oz) glucose
300 g (11 oz) dark (bittersweet) chocolate, melted
White chocolate, melted, then left to set, to decorate

CHARTREUSE MACARON
To make the macaron, mix 150 g (5 oz) of the icing sugar and ground almonds together in a bowl, then pass through a fine sieve into a clean bowl. In a clean, grease-free bowl, whip the egg white until soft peaks form. Add the rest of the icing sugar and beat for 1 more minute. Pour the almond mix over the whipped egg white and using a spatula, stir until the mixture starts to shine. Add the colouring. Part-fill a piping bag fitted with a round nozzle with the mixture and pipe 40 shells on a baking sheet lined with baking paper. Leave at room temperature for about 1½ hours. Preheat the oven to 150°C/300°F/Gas mark 2. Bake the macarons for 10–12 minutes. Leave to cool.

MACARON FILLING
To make the macaron filling, pour the sugar and water into a pan, set over medium heat and bring to 121°C/250°F. Once the sugar/water has reached 115°C/239°F, start beating the eggs in a bowl using an electric whisk. When the sugar/water mixture reaches temperature, pour it over the eggs slowly, and beat using the electric whisk on full speed. Continue to beat until cold. Add the softened butter in 4–5 batches, then flavour as desired.

SPONGE

Preheat the oven to 180°C/350°F/Gas mark 4. Line a Swiss roll tin (jelly roll pan) with baking paper. Line trays that will fit into the refrigerator with baking paper. Place 15 baking rings, each 7 cm (2¾ in), on the trays and line each with acetate strips, 24 x 4 cm (9 x 1¾ in).

To make the sponge, whip the egg whites in a bowl, using an electric beater set on a medium speed until stiff. Add the sugar and whip on full speed for another 1 minute. Add the egg yolks and beat to fully incorporate. Remove the bowl from the mixer. Sift in the flour and fold in gently with a spatula. Spread the sponge mixture evenly in the tin to 1 cm (³/₈ in) thick. Bake for 12–15 minutes. Leave to set in the tin for a few minutes before turning out onto a wire rack to go cold. Stamp out 7 cm (2¾ in) discs from the sponge and place the disc in each ring.

PASTRY CREAM

To make the pastry cream, beat the egg yolks with the sugar in a heatproof bowl. Add the flour and custard powder and stir well. Meanwhile, bring the milk to the boil in a small saucepan, then pour over the egg yolk mixture, stirring constantly. Pour the egg mixture back into the pan and return to the heat. Continue cooking until the cream has thickened. Pour into a container. Cover the top with cling film (plastic wrap) to stop air from getting to the cream. Leave to cool.

CHARTREUSE CREAM

To make the chartreuse cream, whip the cream in a bowl until soft peaks form. Once the pastry cream is cool, warm the chartreuse cream in a pan over low heat and stir in the agar agar. Pour the liqueur over the cold cream then fold in the whipped cream carefully with a spatula. Part-fill a piping bag with the cream mixture and pipe onto the sponge layers. Allow to set for at least 2 hours in the refrigerator.

CHOCOLATE TRUFFLE

To make the chocolate truffle, pour the glucose and 300 ml (½ pint) of the whipping cream into a medium pan, set over medium heat and heat to 90°C/194°F. Pour the melted chocolate over the top. Allow to cool naturally to room temperature. Pour over the rest of the cream, stir in and leave to set in the refrigerator.

GANACHE

To make the ganache, in a medium pan, boil the whipping cream and glucose to 90°C/194°F. Pour over the melted chocolate and leave to cool to room temperature. Remove the cake from the freezer and remove from the ring. Discard the acetate strip then place onto a wire rack. Pour hot ganache over to glaze.

Remove the sponge from the freezer and discard the rings and acetate strips. Place on a wire rack.

Decorate the sides with white chocolate pieces. Fill one half of the macaron with melted chocolate then place another one on top. Gently place over the cake

Vera's Traditional Caribbean Bakery, Birmingham

Owner
Vicky Bennett and daughter Natalie

Size of Business
1 shop, 2 staff

Type of Bakery
Traditional Caribbean bakery selling cakes, patties, hard-dough bread and buns

Established in September 2012 Vera's Caribbean Bakery is run by lifelong baker Vicky, Vera is the family pet name for her. Daughter Natalie helps out at the weekends. Vicky is unique in the area, since she's the only bakery that caters specifically for the West Indian community, a gap in the market she noticed when she moved to the area from London. 'The old people in the community can't travel far for their breads so I decided to open a bakery here,' she said.

Vicky is Indian and married to a Jamaican. After her marriage she learnt Caribbean baking techniques, and Caribbean products are now part of her everyday repertoire, including hard dough bread, spiced buns, Caribbean brown bread, corn bread, rolls, a range of patties, dumplings, jerk chicken, fried fish and a selection of cakes. The patties, buns and hard dough bread are the best sellers.

Vicky is unique in the area, since she's the only bakery that caters specifically for the West Indian community.

Jerk Chicken Patty

MAKES 12 PATTIES

FILLING

3 chicken legs and thighs
3 tablespoons Jamaican jerk seasoning
2 tablespoons curry powder
2 tablespoons olive oil
2 tablespoons cornflour (corn starch)
150 g (5 oz) mixed frozen vegetables, thawed

PASTRY

400 g (14 oz) plain (all-purpose) flour, plus extra for dusting
2 teaspoons salt
250 ml (8 fl oz) ice cold water
5 tablespoons margarine or vegetable fat, chilled
1 egg yolk, beaten
Yellow food colouring (optional)

PASTRY

To make the pastry, mix the flour, salt and water, in a bowl, with a few drops of yellow food colour. Bring the mixture together, knead slightly, then roll it out on a lightly floured surface and fold in the fat. Repeat the rolling and folding 3 times. Chill it overnight, or for at least 30 minutes.

FILLING

Clean the meat and pierce it with a fork so that the marinade seeps in. Place in a non-metallic container and marinate the meat in the jerk seasoning and curry powder for at least 30 minutes or overnight.

Heat a barbecue hotplate or frying pan, heat the oil and cook the chicken until browned and cooked through. Cut up the meat and discard the skin and bones.

Cook the vegetables in a pan with 120 ml (4 fl oz) of water and 2 tablespoons of cornflour, or just enough to thicken. Make sure the mix is not runny or it will burn. Stir the chicken into the vegetable mix.

Preheat the oven to 180°C/350°F/Gas mark 4. Line two baking sheets. Roll out the pastry and stamp out circles with a 15 cm (6 in) cookie cutter. Brush half of each circle of pastry with beaten egg so that the two halves will seal together. Add some of the chicken and vegetable mixture to each pastry round. Fold in half and crimp the edges with a fork. Pierce the top with the fork to let the steam escape. Bake until the pastry is crispy and golden brown, about 35–40 minutes.

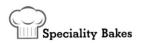

Frost and Snow, Snow Hill, Birmingham

. . . .

Owner/Baker
Pawel Kardaszewski (Coffee Shop and Bakery Assistant) and Catherine Crockford (Café and Bakery Supervisor)

Type of Bakery
Cupcake shop, social enterprise supporting homeless people

Size of Business
1 shop, 4 staff and 10 volunteers

Frost and Snow Bakery is a social enterprise supported by Midland Heart, an organisation that supports people so that they can live independent lives, as well as helping to regenerate communities. The charity creates opportunities for previously homeless people to work in the bakery, and learn skills that will help them get back into work, regain their independence and restore their self-esteem.

The idea began in 2008 when Midland Heart secured a Places of Change Programme grant for a housing development that contained a social enterprise business. Their idea for a mixed living and working development came from charities Common Ground and Greyston, both New York-based organisations, the latter of which produces fine baked goods. Frost and Snow, the bakery and coffee shop opened at Snow Hill in May 2012. To date they have helped more than 70 trainees on the programme and won the Training Journal Awards in 2011 for Best Not-for-Profit Initiative for their innovative programme.

Frost and Snow offer customers a two-day 'taster' to learn about the business, before they go on to complete the 12-week training programme.

Frost and Snow supplied 7000 cupcakes to the London Organising Committee of the Olympic and Paralympic Games.

The charity creates opportunities for previously homeless people to work in the bakery.

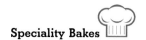

Red Velvet Cupcakes

MAKES 20

115 g (4 oz) butter
280 g (10 oz) caster (superfine) sugar
2 eggs
45 g (1½ oz) unsweetened cocoa powder
1 teaspoon red food colouring
1 teaspoon vanilla extract
240 ml (7¾ fl oz) buttermilk
280 g (10 oz) plain (all-purpose) flour
1 teaspoon bicarbonate of soda (baking soda)
3 teaspoons white vinegar

CREAM CHEESE FROSTING

625 g (1 lb 7 oz) icing (confectioners') sugar
125 g (4½ oz) butter
250 g (9 oz) mascarpone

Preheat the oven to 180°C/350°F/Gas mark 4. Line 2 x 12-hole cupcake trays with paper cases.

CAKE BATTER

In a mixing bowl, beat the butter and sugar until pale and fluffy. Beat in the eggs until the mixture is a thin creamy texture. Stir in the cocoa, colouring and vanilla extract. Scrape down the sides using a spatula and beat the mixture again. Add the buttermilk and flour then beat until smooth. Stir in the bicarbonate of soda and vinegar and beat well. Divide the batter between the paper cases. Bake for 22 minutes, or until risen and a skewer inserted into the centre comes out clean.

CREAM CHEESE FROSTING

To make the frosting, sift the icing sugar into a large bowl and beat in the butter and mascarpone until smooth and well combined. Smooth a dollop over the surface of each, then use a palette knife to quiff the frosting. Break up one of the cakes and sprinkle the crumbs on top of each cupcake.

Baked in Tettenhall, Wolverhampton

. . . .

Owner
Catherine Wyer and Richard Newton (brother and sister)

Type of Bakery
Traditional artisan bakery selling speciality breads, cakes and pastries

Size of Business
1 shop, 6 staff

Baked in Tettenhall is a family-owned artisan bakery, established in September 2012. The driving force behind Baked in Tettenhall is brother and sister duo, Catherine and Richard, with help from mum Margaret, dad Paul, sister Hannah and Catherine's husband Chris. Their average age is just 25. Catherine completed a three-year course in bakery and confectionery at University College Birmingham and has been an avid baker ever since. Richard has had a passion for food from a young age and loves to experiment with new taste combinations to tantalise their customer's taste buds.

The bakery has quickly become an integral part of the local village community and has a loyal customer base. In fact, living in the village has helped the team to understand what it is that their customers want to buy and shaped their product range and development plans. As a result they offer a new and exciting take on the traditional bakery without losing the core value of quality over quantity.

All of their products are made by hand, hence their sales pitch, 'baked with love!' They source all their produce locally and bake on site each day without recourse to preservatives, additives, dough developers or ascorbic acid. Any leftover bread is simply used to create their famous bread puddin'.

They offer a new and exciting take on the traditional bakery without losing the core value of quality over quantity.

Kick in the Walnuts Loaf

MAKES 1 LOAF

400 g (14 oz) strong white bread flour, plus extra for dusting
100 g (3½ oz) wholemeal (whole-wheat) flour
1 generous teaspoon salt
12 g (½ oz) yeast
280 ml (9 fl oz) water
1 scant teaspoon pink peppercorns
½ teaspoon black peppercorns
40 g (1½ oz) raisins
40 g (1½ oz) walnuts
1 teaspoon ground cinnamon

In a bowl, mix the flours, salt, yeast and water together to form a rough dough. Coarsely grind the pink and black peppercorns and add them to the dough along with the raisins, walnuts and cinnamon. Continue kneading until all of the ingredients are dispersed evenly throughout the dough. Leave to rest in a covered bowl for 1 hour. Tip the dough out onto a lightly floured work surface. Shape into an oblong bloomer and place onto a lined baking sheet. Leave to prove for approximately 30 minutes. Meanwhile, preheat the oven to 230°C/450°F/Gas mark 8. Bake for 30–35 minutes.

Mr Bun the Baker, Shropshire

Owner
Terry Satchwill (Owner) and John Coles
(Confectioner)

Type of Bakery
Traditional bakery

Size of Business
1 shop, 10 staff

Owner Terry bought Mr Bun the Baker shop eleven years ago after buying a property near to his daughter's home in Shropshire. He's spent a lifetime in the baking industry and comes from a line of bakers. His grandfather was a baker in World War I in Egypt and Turkey, and his dad used to bake bread for the Co-op in Eastbourne. With his dad, three brothers and sister, the family ran a bakery in Uxbridge, eventually expanding the business to include eight shops. Terry went on to have a successful career owning 13 bakeries across England, and then moved to Miami, where he set up another bakery with his wife. 'We used to buy dumps, build them up and move on', he says. Daughter Claire now runs the shop. John Coles works with Terry, making the confectionery and Mike Saunders is the night baker. Terry now has 1 shop and 10 staff, and supplies some of the farmers markets.

Between them the bakers make 600 rolls every day, and 1500 at a weekend and all by hand. Other specialities include multigrain five seed, the donker loaf, spelt and honey loaf, tomato bread, soft rolls, brownies, flapjacks and fruit pies.

The shop is situated by the beautiful Long Mynd in Shropshire so much of their trade includes hikers and tourists.

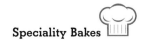

Five-seed Multigrain Loaf

MAKES A 1 KG (2¼ LB) LOAF

300 g (11 oz) wholemeal (whole-wheat) flour
300 g (11 oz) strong white bread flour, plus extra for dusting
2 teaspoons soya flour
25 g (1 oz) oats
25 g (1 oz) barley
25 g (1 oz) rye
2 teaspoons salt

1 teaspoon malt
2 teaspoons easy-blend yeast or 15 g (½ oz) fresh yeast
150 g (5 oz) mixed seeds (golden linseed, pumpkin, sunflower and sesame)
450 ml (¾ pint) tepid water
Vegetable oil, for greasing

Place all the dry ingredients and the yeast in the bowl of an electric mixer, fitted with a dough hook. Add most of the water. Mix on slow speed until the ingredients are incorporated, then increase the speed and mix for approximately 8–10 minutes. Sometimes dough requires a little more or less water than stated so add water with caution. The dough should be soft and pliable. Shape the dough, cover and leave it to rest in a warm place for 1½ hours, or until doubled in size.

Preheat the oven to 180°C/350°F/Gas mark 4. Grease a 1 kg (2¼ lb) loaf tin (pan). Re-shape the dough and place in the tin. Bake for about 45 minutes, or until golden brown. It should sound hollow on the underside when tapped.

Terry went on to have a successful career owning 13 bakeries across England, and then moved to Miami, where he set up another bakery.

Blue Fuchsia, Herefordshire

. . . .

Owner
Jon Brierley (Owner) and Ben Soloman (Assistant)

Size of Business
1 shop, 11 part-time staff

Type of Bakery
Cupcake bakery

Blue Fuchsia is owned by husband and wife team, Jon and Louise. It primarily bakes cakes for the cafe and takeaway as well as making bespoke cakes. The bakery was set up in 2009 when Jon, a stay-at-home dad, decided he wanted to start a business that he could run while still looking after twin children.

Jon has always been interested in baking, so set up a cupcake business from home, selling via the internet and at shows and events. He quickly discovered he had a talent for baking. Not surprisingly he's a self-taught baker who has learned his skills through trial and error.

Blue Fuchsia opened a temporary cupcake shop in Gloucester at the end of 2011. It was successful so he set about looking for a suitable property that could be leased on a longer term and incorporate a cafe into the premises. In August 2012 the Blue Fuchsia Café in Ledbury opened.

The bakery has a very inviting environment and a strong community feel. Some of their customers describe it as 'the pub with no alcohol', or 'the club'. Blue Fuchsia also have a traditional 'stop me and buy one' ice cream bike that they ride around the town in the summer selling ice cream and promoting the bakery.

Ben, Jon's assistant and only 16 years old, is, according to Jon, a very talented young baker. Jon's mother-in-law also works in the bakery and cafe. The family live upstairs.

Jon, a stay-at-home dad, decided he wanted to start a business that he could run while still looking after twin children

Stinking Bishop Cheese Scones

MAKES 8–12

110 g (4 oz) salted butter, frozen or chilled, diced, plus extra
    for greasing
450 g (1 lb) self-raising (self-rising) flour, plus extra for dusting
60 g (2 oz) Parmesan, plus extra for the topping
60 g (2 oz) Stinking Bishop cheese
Pinch of salt
300 ml (½ pint) milk
1 egg, beaten

Preheat the oven to 190°C/375°F/Gas mark 5 Lightly grease a baking sheet.

To the bowl of a food processor add the butter, flour, cheeses and salt. Blitz until the mixture is the consistency of fine breadcrumbs. Add most of the milk and blitz until blended, drizzling in a little more milk until the dough comes together but is not wet. Turn out onto a lightly floured surface and handle as little as possible. Roll out to 2 cm (¾in) deep. Stamp out rounds using a cookie cutter. Place spaced out on the prepared baking sheet, brush with beaten egg wash and dust with Parmesan. Bake for approximately 15 minutes.

Cocorico Pâtisserie, Cardiff

. . . .

Owner/Bakers
Laurian Veaudour (Owner) and Rebecca Coleman
Pastry Chef)

Size of Business
1 shop, 6 staff

Type of Bakery
French pâtisserie – cakes, breads and pastries

The concept of Cocorico Pâtisserie began many years ago in a small village north of Provence called Suze-la-Rousse. Laurian was five years old when he went on a school trip to Boulangerie-Pâtisserie Gondras, one of the two bakeries within the village. He returned home from his trip with the decision that he was going to be a pâtissier and he hasn't faltered from his dream since. Laurian can turn his hands to all types of baking and is an absolute perfectionist.

At the age of 14, Laurian left school and signed up to catering college at Tain l'Hermitage where he was trained by top pastry chefs. He then embarked on a two-year apprenticeship. He moved to Wales twelve years ago, and opened Cocoricco Pâtisserie in 2010. It's been going from strength to strength ever since.

All the cakes, breads and savouries are made from scratch on site with French imported flour. Most of his classic recipes are French; others have been developed and perfected over the years. Laurian found that the locals adapted quickly to his baking style and now he has a long list of customers who book months in advance for his croquembouche.

All the cakes, breads and savouries are made from scratch on site with French imported flour.

Mille Feuille

· ·

SERVES 6

PUFF PASTRY
500 g (1 lb 2 oz) plain (all-purpose) flour, plus extra for
    dusting
1 teapsoon salt
250 ml (9 fl oz) cold water
375 g (13 oz) butter, chilled

PASTRY CREAM
500 ml (17 fl oz milk
1 vanilla pod (bean)
75 g (2 oz) caster (superfine) sugar
4 egg yolks
40 g (1 oz) cornflour (corn starch) or custard powder
Icing (confectioners') sugar, for dusting

PUFF PASTRY

To make the pastry, in a large bowl, mix together the flour, salt and water until you get a dough texture but don't work too much so that it becomes elastic. Turn the dough out onto a lightly floured surface and roll out into a diamond shape. Place the butter in the centre and fold the four corners of the diamond over the butter. Roll the pastry into a rectangle 30 x 90 cm (12 x 35 in). Fold the left side over the centre third, then fold the right side over the top. Turn the pastry 90 degrees. Repeat the last action, fold into a block and then refrigerate for 1½ hours.

Repeat the rolling and folding process another 4 times, then refrigerate again for another 1½ hours. Roll out the pastry to a thickness of 3 mm (1/8 in) Cut the pastry into three even rectangles and place on lightly greased baking sheets.

Preheat the oven to 180°C/350°F/Gas mark 4. Bake the pastry for 20–25 minutes. Leave to set for a few minutes before turning out to go cold on a wire rack.

PASTRY CREAM

To make the pastry cream, pour the milk into a large pan with the vanilla and bring to the boil over medium heat. Meanwhile, in a large bowl, whisk the sugar with the egg yolks until a trail of ribbons form on the surface when the whisk is lifted, and the mixture is pale and fluffy. Whisk in the cornflour. Add the remaining milk and beat to incorporate. Pour the egg mixture into the boiling milk while whisking constantly. Boil for 3 minutes. Tip the custard back into the bowl, cover the surface with cling film (plastic wrap) to prevent a skin forming, then leave to cool. Refrigerate to chill.

Place a layer of pastry on a serving platter. Add a thick layer of custard cream, a layer of pastry, a layer of custard cream and a layer of pastry. Dust the surface with icing sugar.

Welsh Bakery, Haverfordwest

Owners/Bakers
Robert and Brian Davies (father and son)

Type of Bakery
Traditional Welsh Bakery, selling cakes, breads,
traybakes and pasties

Size of Business
2 shops, 25 staff

The Welsh Bakery was bought in 1980 by Brian Davies. He served his apprenticeship in his family's bakery in Merlins Bridge and learnt much from his father. His son Robert has benefited from his father's knowledge, but supplemented his training with study at baking school in Cardiff for two years.

Brian is a more experimental baker then Robert and is always trying new Welsh-inspired flavours. They both take pride in their Welsh origins, are passionate about Welsh food and so the majority of the produce that goes into their baked goods, is sourced locally. It is then created and baked in their bakehouse before being sent out to each of their two shops. Both Robert and Brian believe that they're doing important work for the future of Wales, and hope that they will pass the bakery on to the next generation.

They sell a broad range of products, and unusually their sourdough bread is made with a starter that is sourced from San Francisco.

Both Robert and Brian believe that they're doing important work for the future of Wales

Dragon Bread with Chilli, Coriander and Coconut

MAKES 6

1.35 kg (3 lb) strong white bread flour, plus extra for dusting
30 g (1 oz) salt
30 g (1 oz) bread improver
60 g (2 oz) fresh yeast
1 x 400 ml (14 oz) can coconut milk
450 ml (¾ pint) water

120 g (4 oz) large mixed chillies (medium heat), finely chopped
60 g (2 oz) fresh coriander (cilantro), chopped
190 g (6¾ oz) chilli paste (we use English Provender Very Lazy Red Chillies)
1 egg, beaten, for the egg wash
Olive oil, for brushing

Add the flour, salt, bread improver and yeast to the bowl of an electric mixer. Slowly pour in the coconut milk and water while the mixer is set to the lowest speed. When the dough forms, increase the speed and beat for 5 minutes until a firm dough is formed. Switch off the mixer. Add the chillies, coriander and chilli paste and mix through the dough. Add more flour, if needed, to keep a firm consistency. When the chillies are evenly spread through the dough and the dough feels smooth, tip it out onto a lightly floured tray. Cover and leave to rest for 1½ hours.

Cut the dough into 12 oz (340 g) pieces and shape into round loaves. Return the loaves to the tray, cover and leave to rise for another 20–30 minutes.

Preheat the oven to 230°C/450°F/Gas mark 8. On a lightly floured surface, shape into loaves. Place each on a baking tray. Brush with egg wash. Bake for 20–25 minutes. While still hot, brush lightly with olive oil.

Absolute Treats, Carmarthen

Bakers:
Virginia and Jennifer Buls (mother and daughter)

Size of Business
1 shop, 2 staff

Type of Bakery
Vegetarian bakery selling cakes, cookies,
traybakes and a few pastries

The mother and daughter team are self-taught bakers with a mission to change the way people view baking, exploring recipes that eliminate the need for dairy and eggs. They studied together for their masters degrees in fine art and enjoyed baking and selling cupcakes while they studied. Once they finished their degrees, they decided to set up a vegetarian coffee shop.

The clock tower in which their shop is situated is the only remaining original building of the old Carmarthen market. The shop itself is tiny, but is jam packed with all their own products created from scratch in their home kitchen. All their products are vegetarian and approximately 85 per cent are also vegan friendly.

They make all their own products they are able to adapt their recipes to suit the dietary requirements of their customers. They specialise in dietary specific layer cakes, cupcakes, muffins, sponges and traybakes, plus a range of 15 vegan friendly cookies, but can turn their hands to all types of baking including, biscuits, pies, rolls, pasties, quiches, tarts, pizzas, Welsh cakes, flans, flapjacks and raw cakes and make fresh homemade vegan soups daily.

In 2011 Jennifer won Best Tasting Cupcake, Best Free-From Cupcake and was crowned UK National Cupcake Champion 2011 at the British Baker's magazine competition in London. More recently they successfully organised a vegan street market event in the market square outside their bakery, with producers from all over the UK attending.

The mother and daughter team are self-taught bakers with a mission to change the way people view baking.

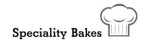

Vegan Chocolate, Almond and Raspberry Brownie with Summer Fruit Coulis

MAKES 1 TRAY

BROWNIE

280 g (10 oz) self-raising (self-rising) flour
90 g (3 oz) ground almonds (almond meal)
180 g (6 oz) caster (superfine) sugar
1 tablespoon baking powder
60 g (2 oz) unsweetened cocoa powder
120 ml (4 fl oz) vegetable oil, plus extra for greasing
230–350 ml (8–12 fl oz) soya or hemp milk
250 g (9 oz) raspberries, plus extra to decorate
35 g flaked (sliced) almonds, to decorate

COULIS

35 g blackberries
35 g raspberries
35 g strawberries
60 g (2 oz) icing (confectioners') sugar

Preheat the oven to 180°C/350°F/Gas mark 4. Grease and line a rectangular baking tray.

BROWNIE

In a large mixing bowl, combine the brownie ingredients, adding enough of the milk to make a gloopy consistency. Add the raspberries last. Whisk thoroughly and quickly for no more than 3 minutes, or the cake will become dense and heavy. Pour the batter into the prepared baking tin. Scatter over the extra raspberries and the flaked almonds. Bake for approximately 20 minutes, if a skewer inserted into the centre comes out clean, the cake is baked. Set aside to cool.

COULIS

Meanwhile, to make the coulis, place all the ingredients into a blender and blend for 2 minutes, or until thoroughly pulped. Force through a sieve into a jug (pitcher). Drizzle the coulis over each brownie just before serving.

THE
CAKE SHOP
BAKERY
EST 1946

PIZZA, BROWNIES,
TARTS, MERINGUES
FROM
WOODBRIDGE, SUFFOLK

South East England

The Cake Shop Bakery, Woodbridge, Suffolk

Owner/Bakers
Peter, Christine, David and Lindsay Wright

Type of Bakery
Third-generation family artisan bakery

Size of Business
1 shop, 20 staff

The Cake Shop Bakery was founded in 1946 by Jonathan and Miriam Wright. In 1970 their son Peter took over with his wife Christine. Now in its third generation, the bakery is run by David with help from his sisters Lindsay, Andrea, Sarah and Sophie. David started working in the bakery from a young age and has always been a keen baker. Before returning to the family business David worked for bakeries in London supplying Harrods and Selfridges department stores.

Lindsay has an artistic flair for presentation and flavour combinations, helped in part by her degree in fine art. Between them, David and his four sisters took over the running of the bakery in 2013. The bakery sells high quality celebration cakes, a range of breads from bloomers to sourdough, and cakes from gingerbread men to lavender brulée tarts. Although David is an all-rounder, he is most commonly found pulling fresh bread from the oven whilse Lindsay takes care of the cakes.

The Cake Shop Bakery is one of the oldest businesses in Woodbridge and remains community-centred. Their philosophy has always been one of constant learning, 'a business as established as ours understands the necessity of progression. Everyday the bakery changes by a small amount. We try to improve things any way we can.'

'We are a real family business, with all the family actually baking.'

THE CAKE SHOP BAKERY

ROSE WATER AND
PISTACHIO MERINGUE
£2.00 N GF V

Honey and Barley Loaf

MAKES 1 LOAF

100 g (3½ oz) wholemeal (whole-wheat) barley flour
100 g (3½ oz) plain (all-purpose) flour
300 g (11 oz) strong white bread flour, plus extra for dusting
1 teaspoon salt
20 g (¾ oz) fresh yeast

1 tablespoon rapeseed oil
25 g (1 oz) honey
1 egg
100 ml (3½ fl oz) milk
Water
Handful of toasted malted oats, seeds or grains, to decorate

By hand: In a bowl, mix the flours together. Add the salt, yeast, oil, honey, egg and milk. Gently mix together into a ball, adding additional flour or water, as needed, to produce a soft, pliable mix. It's better to have the dough on the wet rather than dry side. Tip out onto a lightly floured work surface. Dust some flour onto your hands and begin kneading. When the dough gets too sticky to work comfortably, dust some more flour onto your hands. Continue to knead for 10 minutes.

Using an electric mixer: add all the ingredients to the bowl and start the mixer. Keep checking the dough, adding flour or water as required and continue mixing until the dough becomes springy and clingy. With many mixers the dough clings to the hook and sides in a regular pattern when it is ready.

Cover and set the dough aside in a warm place and allow to prove until doubled in size, about 30 minutes. Knock back (punch down) the dough, shape the loaf and decorate the top by rolling the loaves into the seeds or grains. Mist the loaf with water if the topping doesn't hold then sprinkle on the topping. Prove again until the dough has approximately doubled in size and is light and airy, about 30 minutes.

Preheat the oven to 220°C/425°F/Gas mark 7. Bake for 20 minutes, then turn the loaf and bake for another 10 minutes, or until the bread has a brown crust and a hollow sound when tapped on the base.

Yasar Halim Pâtisserie, Haringey, London

Owner/Bakers
Yasar Halim (owner) Demetrios Charalambous and
Hatice Hudaverdi

Size of Business
2 shops, about 35 staff

Type of Bakery
Turkish Cypriot bakery selling a range of breads,
cakes and savouries

Yasar Halim Pâtisserie is a family-run Turkish Cypriot bakery that was established in 1981 and became an instant success. It is the first bakery of its kind on Green Lanes, the name for the North London borough of Haringey in which the bakery is situated. The bakery sell fresh and hot breads, savouries, including spinach and cheese pastries, traditional pilavuna, pizzas and spicy lahmacun, an assortment of baklava and fresh cream cakes. Most of the recipes made are those of Yasar's mother, and they're all made using traditional Cypriot baking methods. Their produce is loved by Greek and Turkish residents who meet regularly in the shop. Every half an hour, this bakery restocks its shelves with bread fresh from the ovens.

Demetrios is a Cypriot-Greek baker who has worked at Yasar Halim's Pâtisserie for 20 years. He trained at London's Southbank baking school and learnt the majority of his methods at the bakery where he now works. He specialises in wedding cakes and sugarcraft as well as traditional Turkish and Greek pastries and cakes. Hatice is a Cypriot-Turkish baker who has worked at the pâtisserie for 12 years. A former housewife, she decided to develop her natural baking skills by learning on the job.

Most of the recipes made are those of Yasar's mother.

Pilavuna

. . . .

FILLING

100 g (3½ oz) haloumi cheese, grated (shredded)

250 g (9 oz) pilavuna (flaouna) cheese (optional), or
    600 g (1 lb 6 oz) mild Cheddar cheese, grated (shredded)

1 teaspoons dried mint

¼ teaspoon mastic gum

¼ teaspoon mahlab

65 g (2¼ oz) semolina

30 g (1 oz) yeast

30 g (1 oz) plain (all-purpose) flour

2 large eggs, for the filling

3 eggs beaten with 60 ml (2 fl oz) milk, for the egg wash

45 g (1½ oz) sultanas (golden raisins)

120 g (4 oz) sesame seeds

PASTRY

250 g (9 oz) plain (all-purpose) flour, plus extra
    for dusting

30 g (1 oz) unsalted butter

1 teaspoon salt

1 teaspoon sugar

1 teaspoon cinnamon

½ teaspoon mastic gum

½ teaspoon mahlab

30 g (1 oz) yeast

300 ml (½ pint) water

FILLING

Put both cheeses into the bowl of an electric mixer along with the mint, mastic gum, mahlab, semolina, yeast and flour. Mix to combine all the ingredients. Add the eggs and sultanas and continue mixing. Set aside to rest for 30 minutes at room temperature.

PASTRY

Meanwhile, make the pastry. Put all the ingredients, except for the water into the bowl of an electric mixer. Fit a dough attachment, and start mixing, adding the water gradually, then slowly increase the speed. Tip out onto a lightly floured surface and knead the dough into a ball. Slice into 50–55 g (1¾–2 oz) pieces and roll each into smaller balls. Set aside to rest for 10–15 minutes.

Roll out pastry the dough into flat circles 3–5 mm (¹/₈–¼ in thick). Stamp out precise circles using a 10–12.5 cm (4–5 in) pastry cutter and egg wash the top. Place the sesame seeds on the work surface, turn the egg-washed side of the pastry onto the seeds so that they stick to the surface. Egg wash the unseeded sides.

Roll the cheese filling into balls each weighing 150 g (5 oz) and place in the centre of the unseeded side of the pastry circles. Brush the filling with egg wash. Fold the circles over the filling to form parcels. Set aside on a greased baking sheet to rest for 15 minutes to allow the yeast to grow. Meanwhile preheat the oven to 160°C/325°F/Gas mark 3. Bake for 35–40 minutes.

Birdwood Bakery, Leigh-on-Sea, Essex

Owner/Baker
Roseanne Strong (Owner) and Mark Costello
(Head Baker)

Size of Business
3 shops, 1 baking unit, about 30 staff

Type of Bakery
Artisan bakery and café selling a full range of
bread and confectionery

Birdwood Bakery is Southend's only local artisan bakery. From their purpose-built facility they supply their three bakeries.

Owner Roseanne is originally from Australia but moved here 12 years ago, following a holiday to the UK during which she fell in love with the country and decided to stay. She was raised on a remote cattle station in New South Wales, and says the family had to make their own bread every day. Since then Roseanne has travelled the world, picking up new ideas, methods and recipes along the way.

A trained chef, Roseanne opened Birdwood Bakery two years ago and hasn't looked back since. She's helped by Mark, the head baker, who has been baking for three years. This duo have worked together for more than 10 years and Roseanne believes that Mark has a natural flare for flavour and is one of the best bakers in the UK. The recipes they bake to stock their shops are the results of 20 years of experimentation. The sourdough breads are the products that define this bakery, and are made using traditional methods of fermentation and a real starter, which is now four years old. They're so passionate about their sourdough that they refer to the dough process as their 'little mate' – as they feed and water it daily.

Their sourdough flour is stoneground in the UK and is 100 percent organic and yeast free. Their Turkish flatbread is a bestseller and they use it to make delicious sandwiches to sell in the bakeries. The duo also make their own wholemeal puff pastry, which they use to make sausage rolls. Loyal local customers proclaim them to be the best they've ever had. 'We pride ourselves on the interest we have in our products and we have fun inventing new tastes,' says Roseanne.

Roseanne has travelled the world, picking up new ideas, methods and recipes along the way.

Sausage Roll with Lamb and Mango Chutney in Turmeric Pastry

. . . .

MAKES 12

PASTRY

675 g (1½ lb) plain (all-purpose) flour, plus extra for dusting

20 g (¾ oz) salt

20 g (¾ oz) tumeric

635 g (1 lb 6½ oz) butter, chilled

300 ml (½ pint) water

4 teaspoons vinegar

2 tablespoons milk

1 egg, lightly beaten

nigella seeds, to decorate

FILLING

4 onions, finely chopped

½ teaspoon garlic

Olive oil, for frying

3 potatoes, grated (shredded)

3 carrots, grated (shredded)

50 g (1¾ oz) breadcrumbs

4 sprigs of mint, chopped

2 tablespoons massaman Thai curry paste

1 kg (2¼ lb) lean minced (ground) lamb

Salt and pepper, to taste

500 g (1 lb 2 oz) mango chutney

PASTRY

To make the pastry, mix together the flour, salt and tumeric in an electric mixer. Add the 135 g (4½ oz) of the butter and mix through to form breadcrumbs, then add the water and vinegar and continue beating until a smooth dough is formed. Wrap in cling film (plastic wrap) and refrigerate for at least 30 minutes.

FILLING

Meanwhile, to make the filling, fry the onion and garlic in a little olive oil over a medium heat. Tip into a bowl and leave to go cold. Add the potatoes, carrots, breadcrumbs, mint and curry paste and cook until fragrant. Add the lamb mince and season with salt and pepper. Mix to combine.

Preheat the oven to 180°C/350°F/Gas mark 4.

Roll out the dough on a lightly floured surface and place the remaining butter in the centre. Fold the edges of the dough over the butter so that it is completely encased in dough. Roll out the dough with the butter inside. Fold in the edges and roll it out again. Repeat the folding and rolling once more, then roll the dough to 2 mm (¹/₈ in) thick. Transfer the dough to a large, flat baking sheet lined with baking paper. Place the filling in the centre of the pasty in a rectangular shape, like a sausage. Add the mango chutney in a line on top. Fold one half of the pastry over the filling, then repeat with the other side. Seal with water. Mix the milk into the egg to make an egg wash and brush over the pastry. Sprinkle with nigella seeds. Bake for 20 minutes, or until the pastry is golden.

Outsider Tart, Chiswick, London

. . . .

Owners
David Lesniak and David Muniz

Size of Business
1 shop, 10 staff

Type of Bakery
Brownies, cheesecakes, whoopie pies, bread and
typical American treats

Partners David Lesniak (from New York) and David Muniz – aka OD, or Other David – (from Mississippi) started baking for fun when they moved to the UK from America in 2005. After baking for friends, they set up a cake stall at Richmond Farmer's Market. Their popularity grew and the Outsider Tart boys became known for creating some of the most delicious and decadent cakes in London, as well as being the first to introduce the now-ubiquitous whoopie pie to our shores. The Davids are self-taught and although they have had formally trained bakers work with them they have found that passionate, eager, home-taught individuals, who train on the job, make the best team for them. 'We don't stick to any baking rules, rather we experiment and test recipes and create our own unique methods for baking. Our clotted cream baked cheesecake is directly influenced by our location.' They use original American recipes that have been handed down through their families. Taste, flavour and innovation are essential ingredients. From red velvet cakes and coconut cream pies to Lady Baltimore cake and marriage pies, the Davids are at the forefront of an American baking revolution.

The permanent bakery and café, Outsider Tart, opened in July 2009. Outsider Tart is known for its daily changing variety of cakes, cupcakes, cookies, whoopie pies, muffins … the list goes on. 'Our regular customers are more like family members who come for a coffee and a cookie, or tea and slice of cake. The counter in the centre of the bakery acts as a bar or table for visitors.'

Outsider Tart also has a large selection of hard-to-find dry goods from America on sale in the bakery and online.

They have two kitchens underneath their spacious shop front. 'Everyone in Chiswick knows who we are and what we're about – we are fabulous after all.'

Outsider Tart was named a 2010 cultural hotspot by the Observer and voted Cafe/Fast Food Outlet of the Year at the Restaurant & Bar Design Awards 2010.

'Everyone in Chiswick knows who we are and what we're about – we are fabulous after all.'

Turtle Cheesecake

MAKES 1 CHEESECAKE

150 g (5 oz) plain (all-purpose) flour
4 tablespoons unsweetened cocoa powder
¾ teaspoon baking powder
¼ teaspoon salt
115 g (4 oz) unsalted butter, softened, plus extra for greasing
6 tablespoons sugar
2 large egg yolks, lightly beaten

FILLING

900 g (2 lb) cream cheese, softened
340 g (11¾ oz) light brown sugar
½ teaspoon salt

4 large eggs, at room temperature
2 teaspoons vanilla extract
275 g (10 oz) sour cream

TOPPING

450 g (1 lb) sugar
240 ml (8 fl oz) water
240 ml (8 fl oz) double (heavy) cream
60 g (2 oz) butter, unsalted or salted
60 g (2 oz) pecans, chopped
60 g (2 oz) mini chocolate chips (optional)

Preheat the oven to 180°C/350°F/Gas mark 4. Grease and line a 23 cm (9 in) round springform cake tin (pan).

BASE

To make the cookie base, in a large bowl, whisk together the flour, cocoa, baking powder and salt. In another bowl, cream the butter and sugar until fluffy. Slowly add the dry ingredients until evenly distributed then stir in the egg yolks. The mixture will be very crumbly and almost appear dry. Press into the prepared tin and pat it firmly into the base and slightly up the sides. Pierce the surface with a fork in several places. Bake for 15–20 minutes, or until the crust appears firm. Leave to cool slightly before filling.

FILLING

Meanwhile, make the filling. In an electric mixer fitted with a paddle, beat the cream cheese at medium speed until light, about 4 minutes. Add the brown sugar and salt and continue mixing for another 4 minutes. Add the eggs, one at a time, beating well after each addition. Reduce the mixer speed to low. Combine the vanilla and sour cream, then add it to the batter. Pour the batter into the cooled cookie base. Bake for about 60 minutes, or until set. The cake usually rises evenly and cracks around the edges. Cover loosely with foil if it appears to be browning too quickly. The middle will appear jiggly but trust that it is cooked. Let cool completely in the tin to room temperature, then chill in the refrigerator.

TOPPING

Combine the sugar and water in a heavy saucepan. Whisk a little to help dissolve the sugar, then bring to a medium simmer. As the mixture heats, brush the sides of the pan with a wet pastry brush to remove any crystals that form. Do not stir. Once the bubbling syrup starts to take on a caramel colour, watch it closely as it will turn from a beautiful golden caramel to a burnt mess in no time. You're aiming for a deep amber. The whole process can take up to 20 minutes. Remove the pan from the heat and very slowly pour in the cream, whisk to combine, then whisk in the butter until the caramel is creamy and smooth. Let cool before pouring on top of the cheesecake. Decorate with pecans and mini chocolate chips, if using.

Boulangerie Jade, Blackheath, London

Owners
Christophe Le Tynevez and Josua Gerash

Size of Business
2 shops, 22 staff

Type of Bakery
Wide range of breads, cakes, tarts, pastries,
biscuits, macarons

Boulangerie Jade is a fine French bakery and pâtisserie in the heart of Blackheath Village, London. Owner Christophe is a trained French pâtissier who came to the UK 20 years ago to work as a chef. He set up Boulangerie Jade 11 years ago, taking over a traditional English bakery. He claims to be the only French pâtissier in the UK to make his own croissants. Though the mainstay of the bakery are French recipes developed during his apprenticeship in France, Christophe does make and sell traditional British produce, albeit with a French twist. He also makes cakes for special occasions, including the increasingly popular French wedding cake, croquembouche.

Christophe sources ingredients from France and firmly believes in making produce without the use of artificial flavourings. Josua, the pastry chef, has worked at the bakery for the last four years, and adds his own German influence to the baking partnership.

Both Christophe and Josua are perfectionists, firmly believeing that 'taste always comes first'.

'We sell a wide range of fresh products which are not necessarily easy to find in Great Britain such as Paris-Brest, Saint Honore, gallette des rois, Buche de Noel, pain au levain, campaillou bread,' says Christophe. 'We also have a lot of regular customers who come religiously everyday to our bakery. Some say that a lot of our products are better than those they have purchased in France. You can sit down and enjoy a cup of French coffee with any of our delicious products.'

Christophe sources ingredients from France and firmly believes in making produce without the use of artificial flavourings.

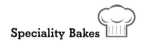

Croquembouche

· ·

MAKES 1 CAKE

CHOUX PASTRY

750 ml (1¼ pints) water
15 g (½ oz) salt
15 g (½ oz) sugar
300 g (11 oz) butter
600 g T45 flour (this is a specialist French pâtisserie flour)
14 eggs
2 beaten eggs, for the egg wash
sugar pearls, to decorate

CREAM FILLING

1 litre (1¾ pints) semi-skimmed (half fat) milk
200 g (7 oz) sugar
1 vanilla pod
8 egg yolks
180 g (6¼ oz) T45 flour

NOUGATINE

1.5 kg (3 lb 6 oz) sugar
150 g (5 oz) glucose
200 ml (7 fl oz) water
300 g (11 oz) flaked (sliced) almonds, to decorate

CHOUX PASTRY

To make the choux pastry, pour the water, salt, sugar and butter into a large pan, place over medium heat and bring to the boil Add the flour in batches while stirring constantly. Cook the dough on high heat for approximately 5 minutes. Tip into the bowl of an electric mixer and mix at low speed until it cools. Slowly add the eggs one at a time to the dough while mixing until it reaches the correct consistency: it should almost fall off a spoon when scooped up and leave a ribbon – not too thick and not too runny. If you add too few eggs the dough will be hard. Preheat the oven to 180°C/350°F/Gas mark 4.

Part fill a piping bag with the pastry dough, and use to pipe small balls, each about 15 g (½ oz) onto a baking sheet. Brush each with egg wash. Gently press the tops with a fork. Bake for 30 minutes, until golden and the pastry balls sound hollow when tapped. Puncture the underside with a skewer and leave to cool in the turned off oven.

CREAM FILLING

To make the cream filling, pour the milk, half the sugar and the whole vanilla pod into a large pan and bring to the boil over medium heat. Stir just to combine. In a separate bowl, combine the rest of the sugar with the egg yolks. Add the flour and whisk very quickly until a smooth paste is formed. The speed ensures it isn't lumpy. If it's lumpy, then the sugar will burn the yolk when heated. Pour the boiled milk into the egg mixture in a steady stream and stir quickly and constantly. Return the mixture to the pan set over high heat and whisk vigorously for 5 minutes, until it is 85°C (185°F). Pour into a tray, smooth evenly, cover with cling film (plastic wrap) and leave to cool. Refrigerate to chill.

NOUGATINE

To make the nougatine, combine the sugar, glucose and water in a large pan set over medium heat and stir. Lightly wipe the sides of the pan with a wet brush to prevent crystallisation when heating. Cook for 15–20 minutes until light golden brown and caramelised at 140°C/284°F. Set aside 500 g (1 lb 2 oz) of caramel to build the croquembouche. Add flaked almonds to the rest and smooth evenly in a lightly greased baking tray. Leave on a rack to cool but not for long enough to allow it to set.

The nougatine is now approximately 100°C/212°F so you must work very fast before it sets. Pastry chefs are experienced at work with this hot substance. Home cooks can purchase special gloves for working with nougatine. Make sure that the work surface and all equipment is oiled well so that nothing sticks. Roll out the nougatine, even the sides with an oiled flat knife and cut out diagonal/triangular strips. Line the loose base of a cake tin that is the diameter of the base of the croquembouche with a whole piece of nougatine. Trim away the excess. Use a pastry (cookie) cutter to cut circles and crescents from the rolled nougatine for the top decoration of the croquembouche.

MAKING THE CHOUX BUNS

Place the profiteroles on baking paper, pierce holes in the base of each using a skewer. Mix the pastry cream on a high speed. Use to part fill a piping bag and use to fill the profiteroles. Reheat the caramel that has been set aside in a pan to 140°C/284°F Carefully dip the top of each choux bun into the caramel and finish each with a sugar pearl.

ASSEMBLING THE CROQUEMBOUCHE

Select the largest profiteroles for the nougatine base. Dip the base of each in melted caramel and stick around the circumference of the base. The caramel adds strength to the structure. Continue dipping one edge of each choux bun in the nougatine and using the dipped edge to stick to the layer below. As you assemble the layers set the choux buns so that they will taper as a spire to a point. Be careful to get the right profiterole shapes together so they fit and make a stable pyramid.

Add stamped nougatine shapes as desired, attaching them with nougatine. Finally, using a whisk, flick caramel at high speed from side to side to make a wispy 'angel's hair' effect and wind it round the finished pyramid.

Cinnamon Square, Rickmansworth, Hertfordshire

Owner/Bakers
Paul Barker (Owner) and Hazel Carmichael

Type of Bakery
Artisan bakery, shop and café that offers baking masterclasses and teaches children the science behind baking

Size of Business
1 shop, 26 staff

Cinnamon Square was opened in 2005 by Paul and his wife Tricia. Paul is a trained and professional master baker and takes a scientific view of his trade. He's obtained academic qualifications in baking, cake decorating, pâtisserie and flour milling. By the end of his studies, he had completed every course and module available.

Paul regards his shop as the 'theatre of baking' since the produce is made in view of the customers in 'The Makery', Cinnamon Square's scientific baking laboratory. Customers can see, listen, touch, smell and taste the whole experience. 'We're creative, forward-thinking and work hard to continuously improve the customer experience,' says Paul. 'We have a sourdough smell-ometer, created the Circle of Loaf visual to explain its process and create fun experiments during children's parties so that children can find out about the science of baking.'

Paul teaches adults and children to bake and make bread, cakes, pâtisserie and chocolates. Since opening, he has taught more than 10,000 children.

The recipes used at Cinnamon Square originate from a variety of sources, including some that are more than 100 years old, as well as ideas adapted from Paul's 30 years of bakery experience, and from his working in many different parts of the world.

The Cinnamon Square bun, the bakery's speciality bake, is a sweet fermented bun, rolled in cinnamon and topped with cream cheese frosting has won them a Great Taste Award. Their Ricky sticky bun, a product named after the town in which the company is based, won the Speciality Category at the World Bread Awards in 2013.

Hazel joined Cinnamon Square in 2006 and works alongside Paul to produce exquisite pâtisserie and savouries.

The Cinnamon Square bun, the bakery's speciality bake, is a sweet fermented bun, rolled in cinnamon and topped with cream cheese.

Cinnamon Square Buns

MAKES 8 BUNS

PASTRY

600 g (1 lb 6 oz) strong white bread flour, plus extra for dusting
50 g (1¾ oz) sugar
10 g (¹⁄₃ oz) salt
50 g (1¾ oz) unsalted butter, softened at room temperature
15 g (½ oz) skimmed milk powder
300 ml (½ pint) water
20 g (¾ oz) yeast

CINNAMON FILLING

200 g (7 oz) sugar
100 g (3½ oz) butter
2 teaspoons ground cinnamon

CREAM CHEESE FROSTING

100 g (3½ oz) cream cheese
250 g (9 oz) icing (confectioners') sugar
30 g (1 oz) butter, softened

Line two 23 cm (9 in) square baking tins (pans).

PASTRY

In a large bowl, mix together the flour, sugar, salt, butter, milk powder, water and yeast until a smooth cream is formed. Do not over-mix or it will break down to a liquid. Roll out the dough on a lightly floured surface into a rectangle 56 x 28 cm (22 x 11 in).

CINNAMON FILLING

To make the cinnamon filling, blend all the ingredients in a mixing bowl until a paste is formed. Spread evenly over the dough, then roll up the dough evenly into a sausage. Trim the dough into 8 even pieces and place four into each prepared tin. Seal inside a lidded plastic tub and allow to rise for 40–50 minutes.

Preheat the oven to 200°C/400°F/Gas mark 6. Bake for 8–10 minutes, until golden brown. When removing the tins from the oven, bang them on a heatproof surface, to prevent the buns from collapsing. Leave to set for a few minutes before turning out onto a wire rack to go cold.

CREAM CHEESE FROSTING

Mix the cream cheese frosting ingredients together in a large bowl. Spread a generous layer on each bun.

The Vintage Cake House, Farnham, Surrey

Owner/Bakers
Natalie Steward and Annabel Mountford

Size of Business
1 shop, 6 staff

Type of Bakery
Wide range of cakes, traybakes and pastries

True to its name The Vintage Cake House is a bakery and tearoom with a penchant for a bygone era. Each month, owners and bakers Natalie and Annabel run themed days in their vintage-style tearoom in Farnham. Together they celebrate different eras from the 1920s to the 1960s and sell the produce of those eras in the cake shop, while dressed appropriately in the style of the times. The shop specialises in homemade cakes, cream teas, loose-leaf tea and all things vintage.

They've only been open for a year but already feel established in the community. Owner Natalie turned down the opportunity to go to university so that she could start her own business. 'After helping start a small wedding cake business in Nottingham I knew I wanted to become self-employed and open my own vintage style tearoom and cake shop', she says. 'After long, late nights struggling through a business plan, juggling a full-time job, finding the perfect premises and endless meetings with the bank I was finally granted the funds I needed to open The Vintage Cake House.

The duo are predominately self-taught bakers, though Natalie has always loved baking and comes from a family of cooks. Annabel is a home baker whose strength is pastry and bread. She likes to experiment with flavours and enjoys watching the customers indulge in her decadent cakes. They each have a different approach to baking, with Natalie working by eye when measuring ingredients, while Annabel likes to be exact.

All of the produce sold in the tearoom and shop is made on site. They also make celebration cakes to order. 'The fact we are completely independent and have such a unique style makes us different from anywhere else in Farnham,' they say.

They each have a different approach to baking, with Natalie working by eye when measuring ingredients, while Annabel likes to be exact.

Vintage Rose Cake

MAKES 1 CAKE

SPONGE

225 g (8 oz) unsalted butter, plus extra for greasing
225 g (8 oz) sugar
4 eggs
2 teaspoons pink food colouring
2 teaspoons rosewater
225 g (8 oz) self-raising (self-rising) flour
1 teaspoon baking powder
Sugared rose petals, to decorate

BUTTERCREAM

225 g (8 oz) butter, softened
1 teaspoon rosewater
250–275 g (9–10 oz) icing (confectioners') sugar

Preheat the oven to 180°C/350°F/Gas mark 4. Grease and line a 20 cm (8 in) cake tin (pan).

SPONGE

In a large bowl, whisk the butter and sugar until light in colour. Add the eggs and continue whisking until light and fluffy. Add a few drops of the food colour and the rosewater and mix well. Sift in the flour and baking powder from a height to ensure there is plenty of air in the mixture. Fold in using a metal spoon, until just mixed. Spoon into the prepared tin. Bake for 45–50 minutes, or until the cake springs back when pressed lightly on top. Leave to set in the tin for 5 minutes before turning out onto a wire rack to cool completely.

BUTTERCREAM

To make the buttercream, beat the butter in a large bowl. Add the rosewater and stir through. Sift in the icing sugar in batches and beat with an electric beater until white in colour. You might not need all of the icing sugar. Spread over the cake and decorate with sugared rose petals.

Victoria Bakery, Barnet, North London

Owners
James and Debbie Freeman, and Kevin Hancy
(Head Baker)

Size of Business
2 shops, about 30 staff

Type of Bakery
Traditional craft bakery selling breads, cakes,
pastries, tarts and traybakes

Victoria Bakery is owned and run by James and Debbie Freeman, the fifth generation of master bakers to run this bakery. The business was started by James' great-great grandfather Robert Freeman, in 1827, in nearby Highgate.

James recalls that his earliest memories are of helping his dad put jam in the doughnuts and standing on a wobby stool to stack the bread. The majority of the bakery's recipes have passed down the generations too. Traditional methods, such as overnight fermentation of bread dough and baking bread on the stone floor of the oven are essential to 'produce really tasty crusty bread', says James. Despite the fact that James has been baking all his life, he continues to learn and recently enrolled on an artisan bread-making course, in order to extend the range of breads he offers for sale.

All of this bakery's produce is baked on site and by hand. The range includes traditionally fermented breads, such as sourdoughs, as well as cakes, savouries and sandwiches. James tries to source all produce that goes into the bakes locally.

Kevin, the head baker, is highly respected by the team. Also a highly skilled master baker, he has worked with James for the last 17 years.

The business philosophy is to provide 'quality service second to none'.

London Bloomer Loaf

MAKES 2 LOAVES

SOURDOUGH STARTER
150 g (5 oz) strong white bread flour
150 ml (6 fl oz) water

SPONGE STARTER
400 g (14 oz) strong white bread flour
200 ml (7 fl oz) water
1 g yeast

BREAD DOUGH
12 g (½ oz) salt
20 g (¼ oz) yeast
1½ teaspoons rapeseed oil
740 g (1 lb 10 oz) strong white bread flour
75 g sourdough starter (see recipe)
450 g (1 lb) sponge (see recipe)

SOURDOUGH STARTER
To make a sourdough starter, lightly mix 50 g (1¾ oz) flour with 50 ml (2 fl oz) water in a large mixing bowl. Cover the bowl and leave in a cool place. Over each of the next 3 days add the same quantites of flour and water to the mix, stirring just to combine. The starter should have bubbles on the surface and a slightly acidic aroma.

SPONGE STARTER
To make a sponge starter, thoroughly mix the ingredients in a bowl to develop the gluten. Cover and leave to ferment for 24 hours in a warm place.

BREAD DOUGH
To make the bread dough, add the sourdough starter and the sponge to the other ingredients in a large bowl. Add the salt and yeast separately. Mix well to develop the gluten. Rest for at least 30 minutes before using.

Divide into two equal pieces. Shape into rounds, set aside to rest for 10 minutes, then shape into long bloomers. Place the dough pieces smooth side down on to a lightly floured surface, stretch and flatten into an oval, fold the two edges into the centre and press down. Then fold the bottom edge into the middle and press down, rpeat with the top edge to make a long sausage shape. Cover with a cloth and prove for 30 minutes in a warm place.

Score each diagonally with 13 cuts just before baking. Meanwhile, preheat the oven to 230°C/450°F/Gas mark 8 and add a tray of water to the base of the oven. Put the bread on baking sheets and bake. Open the oven door briefly after 15 minutes to relase any steam. Bake for a further 25–30 minutes until the bread base sounds hollow when tapped.

Cloud 9 Bakery, Brighton

• •

Owner/Bakers
Hannah and Paul McGrath

Size of Business
1 shop and 5–6 staff

Type of Bakery
Quirky cake shop in the centre of Brighton

In the spring of 2010 Hannah and Paul McGrath gave up their London jobs and headed south for sunny Brighton, with a dream of setting up a bakery. Their mission was to make the best cakes in Brighton. The bakery they established trades 50 percent in ice creams and 50 per cent in cakes. 'Brighton is very seasonal,' they say, 'we sell more cakes, coffees and Belgian waffles in the winter and more ice cream in the summer.'

They define their baking style as 'fun, homemade and not too fussy', with Hannah making the cakes, cupcakes and celebration specialities and Paul making the ice cream.

They only use the best natural ingredients in their products saying, 'you won't find any horrible artificial mass produced item in our shop thank you very much!' Everything is made fresh everyday on the premises. Their signature bake is the rainbow cake, originally made to celebrate Brighton Gay Pride. 'The rainbow cake is a traditional vanilla recipe, baked in five thin layers with icing inbetween. When you cut it you see all of the colours.'

Cloud 9 came second in the Best Café category at the 2012 Brighton Foodie Awards.

They only use the best natural ingredients in their products saying, 'you won't find any horrible artificial mass produced item in our shop thank you very much!'

Rainbow Cake

• •

MAKES 1 LARGE CAKE

SPONGE
210 g (8½ oz) whole eggs
350 g (12 oz) caster (superfine) sugar
210 g (8½ oz) butter, softened
140 ml (4½ fl oz) milk
1 teaspoon vanilla extract
350 g (12 oz) self-raising (self-rising) flour
15 g baking powder

5 food colours (pink, green, blue, yellow and purple)
Mini smarties, for decoration

BUTTERCREAM
450 g (1 lb) butter, softened
600 g (1 lb 6 oz) icing (confectioners') sugar, sieved
½ tablespoon vanilla extract

Preheat the oven to 180°C/350°F/Gas mark 4. Grease and line five 23 cm (9 in) loose-base sandwich tins (pans).

SPONGE
To make the cake, in a large bowl, mix the eggs and sugar until pale and creamy. Add the butter and beat the mixture until thick and creamy. Meanwhile, warm the milk and vanilla together in a microwave until lukewarm, or in a small pan over low heat. Sift the flour and baking powder into the egg mixture and fold in slowly until just combined. Slowly pour in the warmed milk and vanilla while mixing. Stir until pale and fluffy. Divide the batter evenly between five bowls. Add a few drops of a different food colour to each bowl and mix until each is uniformly tinted. Tip each batter into a different prepared tin and level the top. Bake all the cakes at the same time, for 10 minutes. Leave to set in the tins for a few minutes, before turning out on to a wire rack to go cold.

BUTTERCREAM
To make the buttercream, in a large bowl, beat the butter and add the icing sugar a little at a time until pale and fluffy. Add the vanilla and mix again. Decide on the order you would like to assemble the rainbow cake. Place the bottom layer on a serving plate and spread buttercream in a thin, even layer over the surface. Place the next cake on top, and coat the top with buttercream as before. Repeat until all the layers are assembled and stacked, then slowly spread the remaining icing around the sides and top of the cake. Smooth the icing by dipping a knife in hot water and smoothing over the surface, then decorate the border with mini smarties.

1066 Bakery, Hastings, East Sussex

· ·

Owners/Bakers
Darren Trevett

Size of Business
5 retail outlets, 65 staff

Type of Bakery
Traditional, artisan bakery

Owner Darren is a self-confessed bread-a-holic. 'It's in the blood, we were brought up around it. I love getting a crusty sourdough loaf out of the oven!' he says. In fact, it's the sourdough that defines this bakery. Initially set up by this grandfather more than 60 years ago, the bakery is now run by the third generation including Darren, his sister Tara and brother Ben. Many of the recipes that they make and sell were developed by Darren's grandfather, but they are also known for developing new tastes and flavours such as their award-winning Cheddar cheese and ale sourdough, and sultana and fennel loaf.

It's not only the recipes that they love experimenting with, the family recently opened up a bakery and café in a classic double-decker bus as an additional outlet to their three cafés, called Mr Bean Coffee House, which sell some of their famous bakes.

Their bestsellers include Eccles cakes, custard Danish pastries, sausage and caramelised onion rolls, and cheese and bacon scones.

'Hastings is a fantastic, vibrant place and we are proud to be part of that. With the next generation of our family keen to bake, we hope to be able to carry on serving our fresh, local products for years to come.'

Many of the recipes that they make and sell were developed by Darren's grandfather.

Cheddar Cheese and Ale Bread

MAKES 1 LOAF

BREAD

465 g (1 lb ½ oz) quick sourdough starter (*see recipe*)
10 g (1/3 oz) salt
260 g (9¼ oz) strong white bread flour, plus extra for dusting
70 g (2¾ oz) wholemeal (whole-wheat) flour
75 ml (3 fl oz) ale
70 g (2¾ oz) mature Cheddar cheese

QUICK SOURDOUGH STARTER

200 ml (7 fl oz) milk
200 ml (7 fl oz) natural (plain) yogurt
100 g (3½ oz) wholemeal (whole-wheat) flour
100 g (3½ oz) strong white bread flour

SOURDOUGH STARTER

To make the sourdough starter, mix the milk and yogurt together in a glass bowl. Put a lid on the bowl but don't seal it completely, to allow the gasses to develop. Put in a warm place for 24 hours, until the yogurt and milk separate forming a large curd. Add the flour, stirring it all back together. Return to a warm place for 3–5 days; stirring daily. It will bubble and have the odour of fermentation and is then ready to use. Return it to the refrigerator if you want to store it, otherwise leave it for 24 hours and use again. Remember that the starter is a living thing and needs to be fed regularly. Every 3–4 days remove about one-third of the mix and top it up with equal amounts of flour and water (for example, if you remove 200 g (7 oz) add back in 100 g (3½ oz) flour and 100 ml (3½ fl oz) water). Once fed, keep at room temperature for 2–3 hours before returning it to the refrigerator.

BREAD

To make the bread, mix together all the ingredients, except for the cheese, in an electric mixer fitted with a dough hook, for 2 minutes on slow speed. Increase to medium speed for about 6 minutes until the dough is well mixed and when removed from the bowl, it is stretchy. Fold in the cheese and leave the dough in the mixing bowl for about 30 minutes to 1 hour, covered in cling film (plastic wrap), in a warm place. Tip the dough onto a lightly floured surface and knock back (punch down) the dough. Knead into shape and put the dough in a proving basket with the bread seam on top, or in a baking tin (pan) with the bread seam underneath. Leave the dough overnight, covered, until it has doubled in volume (about 10–12 hours).

Preheat the oven to 230°C/450°F/Gas mark 8.

Turn the dough out onto a baking sheet or leave in the tin and make several slashes on top of the loaf. Put some ice cubes in a baking tray in the base of the oven. This will melt and make steam and give your loaf a beautiful shine. Bake the bread for 20 minutes, remove the tray from the base of the oven, turn the loaf and continue baking for about 10 minutes, or until the loaf is golden brown and it sounds hollow when tapped underneath.

Tip: Do not feed the starter just before you are about to use it, always take what you need and then feed it. Starters can be frozen.

Champs Bakery, Whitstable, Kent

Owner/Bakers
Geoff and Keith Champs (father and son)

Size of Business
1 shop, 8 staff

Type of Bakery
Small traditional baker and sandwich bar

Geoff has owned Champs bakery for more than 25 years, though it's been in existence for more than 100 years. Dad Keith originally ran a bakery in Birchington, Kent, and Geoff grew up living above it. He left there in 1988 to buy his own bakery. Although Keith is now retired he helps out in the shop whenever he's needed. Geoff can't remember a time when his father didn't have dough in his hands. Geoff has been baking so long that he no longer needs to weigh out his ingredients, he just uses the palm of his hand and guestimates everything. He says baking is in his blood and he knows by looking whether something will work.

Geoff went to college to train to be a baker and then continued to learn his trade on the job. Dad advised him to work for other bakeries before coming into the family shop. Like his father he can turn his hands to all types of baking and is now a master baker.

Despite being a traditional bakery, Geoff is extremely experimental and can often be found on a Saturday morning playing with flavours and methods to create new tastes for his loyal customers. He's rightly proud of the traditional products that he makes. 'We've always just been true to ourselves and baked what our locals wanted,' he says.

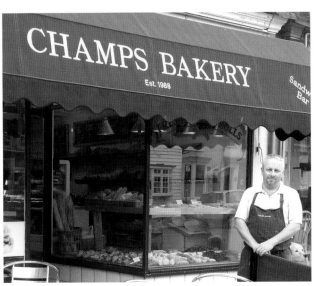

'We've always been true to ourselves and baked what our locals wanted.'

Olive and Roasted Pepper Flatbread

MAKES 8 LOAVES

BREAD

1.8 kg (4 lb) strong white bread flour, plus extra for dusting
60 g (2 oz) yeast
150 ml (¼ pint) olive oil
1 litre (1¾ pints) warm water
60 g (2 oz) salt

FILLING

250 g (8 oz) mixed black and green olives
120 g (4 oz) roasted red peppers
120 g (4 oz) sun-dried tomatoes, chopped
Pinches of dried rosemary, oregano and basil
Cherry tomatoes, to garnish
Olive oil, to drizzle

BREAD

To make the bread, mix the flour, yeast, olive oil, warm water and salt together in a large bowl to make a dough. Turn it out on to a lightly floured work surface and knead it for 5 minutes, then add the olives, roasted red peppers, sun-dried tomatoes and herbs. Set aside in a covered bowl to rest in a warm place for 1 hour, then divide into 8 equal portions and loosely shape each into a small loaf. Set aside to rest again for 30 minutes then, using a rolling pin, roll out into flat ovals. Prove again for 30 minutes (depending on the temperature) until risen in volume and decorate with cherry tomatoes.

Preheat the oven to 210°C/410°C/Gas mark 6½. Place the bread on a baking sheet and bake for 20 minutes, until golden brown. Drizzle with olive oil while hot.

South West England

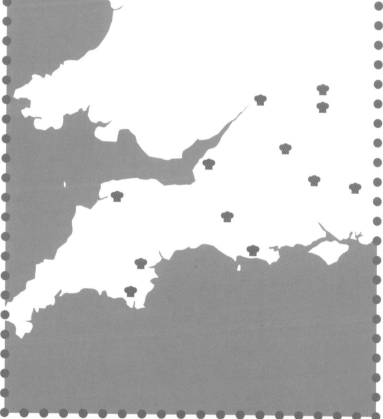

The Phoenix Bakery, Weymouth, Dorset

Owner/Bakers
Aidan and Lisa Chapman (Owners) Tom Robinson
(Baker)

Size of Business
1 shop, 6 staff

Type of Bakery
Artisan Bakery selling breads, savouries and
cakes

Aidan has been baking for more than 25 years and his career includes two years as head baker at The Celtic Bakery in London. While he was there he was inspired by the organic movement and took the opportunity to showcase his artisan breads to an appreciative audience at local farmers markets. The experience proved inspirational and from that point forward Aidan vowed to treat every bakery shop window like a market stall, full of vibrant, seasonal and local products with the intention of creating a show-stopping display to entice every customer.

Aidan moved to Dorset in 2005 and soon after established The Phoenix Bakery with his wife Lisa. True to his word the shop window always displays a fine array of baked goods, while inside the bakery houses a wooden table behind which customers can watch the bakers while they work. He describes The Phoenix as an artisan bakery making and selling breads, cakes, pastries and savouries. The bakery uses local and organic produce and has a coffee shop. All breads are made using the sourdough method with natural wild yeast, long fermentation, high hydration and a low salt content. The result is a long lasting bread with a great taste that is incredibly good for the digestion. 'One of the many things that I love about baking is that you have to use your imagination,' says Aidan, a hands-on experimental baker. Tom has been working with Aiden for 6 months and describes himself as a methodical baker who works in a traditional way. The two complement each other well and although they've worked together for a short time they're already finishing off each other's sentences!

The Phoenix has a bakery school that operates on a Monday, and on Friday night those keen enough can work a whole night shift. Aidan has appeared on the River Cottage television programme a number of times and he is the teacher for all the River Cottage bread courses at their headquarters. He is also an ambassador for the real bread campaign, which fights for the rightful recognition of real bread as a healthy food and a time-honoured trade. Aidan likes to be known as the dough anarchist in his tireless fight to bring real bread back to its rightful place on the table.

Aidan likes to be known as the dough anarchist in his tireless fight to bring real bread back to its rightful place on the table.

Black Garlic and Scapes Sourdough

MAKES 3

BREAD DOUGH

500 g (1 lb 2 oz) strong white bread flour, plus extra for
   dusting
150 ml ¼(pint) sourdough starter (see recipe)
350 ml (12 fl oz) cold water
5 g sea salt mixed with a little water
1 whole bulb black garlic, roughly chopped
6 garlic scapes (curling tops of the garlic bulb), chopped

SOURDOUGH STARTER

500 g (1 lb 2 oz) strong white bread flour
500 ml (17 fl oz) water

SOURDOUGH STARTER

To make the sourdough starter, in a bowl, mix 50 g (1¾ oz) of the flour with 50 ml (2 fl oz) of cold water, cover and leave for 24 hours. Repeat this every day for 10 days, mixing the freshly weighed flour with the same quantity of cold water and adding it to the previous day's mix. It will be bubbly and have an alcoholic aroma. Store it in the refrigerator until required and for up to two weeks. The day before you want to make bread, you need to feed this mixture with one handful of flour and an equal amount of water. Leave at room temperature for 8 hours.

BREAD DOUGH

To make the bread, put the flour into a large bowl. Make a well in the centre and pour the sourdough starter and water into the well. Bring everything together as gently as you can using your hand, until the liquid and flour are just merged. Cover with a clean cloth and leave to rest for about 40 minutes.

Add the salt water and gently mix into the dough. Add the black garlic and 5 garlic scapes and mix in as gently as you can. Cover and refrigerate for at least 18 hours. Remove from the refrigerator and fold the dough. Set aside to rest for 2 hours at room temperature.

Dust a proving basket or banneton with flour, then shape the dough into a round loaf and place it in the basket, seam side up. Prove for 3 hours.

Preheat the oven to 230°C/450°F/Gas mark 8. Line a baking sheet with parchment paper. Gently knock your dough on to the sheet. Take the remaining garlic scape and cut in half. Push the bottom half into middle of dough. Place into the pre-heated oven. Spray the oven with water to create steam and bake for 25 minutes, turning once. Remove from the oven, take out the garlic scape out and push the other half scape in. Bake for another 5 minutes – the steam from the bread will cook the scape.

Tip: Replace the black garlic with standard garlic and the scape with chives, if you like.

Cake Box, Yeovil, Somerset

Owner/Bakers
Andy Egan and step-daughter Leanne Colley

Type of Bakery
Traditional bakery, specialising in traditional cakes,
breads and pastries

Size of Business
1 shop, 9 staff

Cake Box is a family craft bakery that produces everything on site and by hand. The bakery has been on the same site since 1960 and the Egan family have owned it since 1988. Andy trained at college as a baker and has worked in a range of bakeries across Devon and Somerset where he developed his skills. Step-daughter Leanne has been working in the bakery since she was 16. She specialises in confectionery, but like Andy, can turn her hand to all types of baking. They've been working together for 25 years and get on well, which is just as well since Andy says, 'I'm never going to retire, I'll be baking 'til I die'.

The majority of their recipes have been gathered over time and from various sources. For example, Andy's speciality is Australian crunch, a recipe that he's spent years developing. It began as a special request from a customer and now it's the bakery's most popular product. The recipe came from a school canteen. Leanne says people travel from far and wide to buy their traditional cakes such as Battenberg. The Egan family are an integral part of the local community and rely heavily on their trade. The majority of their customers are loyal long-time supporters.

The Egan family are an integral part of the local community.

Australian Crunch

MAKES 30 SQUARES

400 g (14 oz) sugar
310 g (11 oz) margarine
160 g (5¼ oz) lard
2 eggs
450 g (1 lb) plain (all-purpose) flour
225 g (8 oz) desiccated (dry unsweetened shredded)
   coconut

115 g (4 oz) golden (light corn) syrup
Pinch of salt
30 g (1 oz) baking powder
60 g (2 oz) cocoa powder
60 g (2 oz) drinking chocolate
225 g (8 oz) crushed cornflakes
750 g (1 lb 10 oz) plain (semi-sweet) or milk chocolate

Preheat the oven to 360°F/180°C/Gas mark 4. Grease and line a 38 x 23 cm (15 x 9 in) baking sheet with baking paper.

In a large bowl, cream the sugar, margarine, lard and eggs together. Add the rest of the ingredients, except for the chocolate, and mix until combined. Spread the mixture out onto the lined baking sheet using wet hands to stop it sticking. Bake for 25 minutes and cut into 30 squares as soon as it comes out of the oven. Set aside to go cold.

Break the chocolate into chunks and place in a bowl. Set the bowl over a pan of gently simmering water until melted. Stir occasionally. Spread the chocolate over the top of the squares. Cut again when cooled.

Corrister & White, Clevedon, North Somerset

Bakers
Fern Coster and Diane Corrister

Type of Bakery
Celebration cakes and traybakes

Size of Business
1 shop, 12 staff

This mother and daughter team, Diane and Fern, have an online cake business as well as a bespoke cake boutique and café. They call themselves a 'fledgling' business, which they say allows them the opportunity to try different ideas.

Mum Diane has always made cakes for family and friends, including customised special occasion cakes. When her six children left home, she set up a business baking and selling cakes. Diane's recipes developed over years of catering for a large and busy family. Their products are inspired by Australian, English and American recipes. 'To bake great cake you need to use great ingredients,' says Fern.

The original business was established in Newport, which has now become a quiet haven for the team to focus on cake decoration, classes and cake collection. Premises in Clevedon facilitate a cafe and cake boutique, which serves tea, coffee, cakes and sandwiches.

Fern has learnt all her skills from her mother and admits she was a terrible baker in her youth. They describe themselves as 'good basic cooks' that stick to the recipe. 'We don't do crazy flavours but we love to experiment.'

'It enhances our belief that to bake great cake you need to use great ingredients... no margarine for us!'

Victoria Sponge

MAKES 1 LARGE CAKE

SPONGE
Caster (superfine) sugar (an equal weight to the eggs)
Butter (an equal weight to the eggs), plus extra for greasing
5 eggs (weigh eggs in shell to nearest 15 g/½ oz)
Self-raising (self-rising) flour (an equal weight to the eggs)
1 teaspoon good quality vanilla extract
Icing (confectioners') sugar, for dusting

RASPBERRY JAM (JELLY)
200 g (7 oz) fresh raspberries
200 g (7 oz) caster (superfine) sugar
4 tablespoons cassis
1½ teaspoons arrowroot

BUTTERCREAM
100 g (3½ oz) white chocolate
300 g (11 oz) icing (confectioners') sugar
200 g (7 oz) butter
2 teaspoons vanilla extract

Preheat the oven to 150°C/300°F/Gas mark 2. Grease and line three sandwich tins (pans) each 20 cm (8 in) in diameter.

SPONGE
Cream the butter and sugar together, in a bowl, with a spatula, until the mixture has lightened to a pale gold and the batter is very fluffy. Break the eggs into a glass, one at a time, and beat with a fork. Add to the butter and sugar mixture gradually, ensuring each addition is thoroughly absorbed before adding more egg to avoid curdling. If it curdles add a handful of flour and mix in. Gently fold in the flour and add the vanilla. Do not over-mix at this stage. Pour one-third of the mixture into each prepared tin. Bake for 20 minutes, or until they bounce back to the touch. Leave to set for a few minutes then turn out on to a wire rack to go cold.

RASPBERRY JAM (JELLY)
Meanwhile, make the raspberry jam. Put the raspberries, sugar, and cassis in a pan and set over gentle heat until the sugar dissolves, then turn up the heat and bring to a rapid boil. Allow to bubble until the fruit is soft but not too mushy – the liquid should have reduced and thickened slightly. Mix the arrowroot with a little water to make a runny paste and add to the saucepan and mix in. The jam should thicken and become clear. Tip the jam into a clean bowl and cover the top of the jam with cling film (plastic wrap). Pierce to allow steam to escape and leave to cool.

BUTTERCREAM
To make the buttercream, melt the white chocolate in bowl set over a pan of gently simmering water. Leave to cool. Beat the icing sugar, butter and vanilla together at high speed in a mixer until very light and smooth. Mix in the chocolate and stir well.

To assemble the cake, put one sponge on a serving plate, coat the top with jam, then a layer of buttercream. Coat the underside of a second cake with jam and place jam-side down on the buttercream. Top the cake with another layer of jam and a layer of buttercream. Coat the underside of the final sponge with jam, place jam-side down on the buttercream. Finally, dust the top of the cake with icing sugar.

Burbidge's Bakery, Andover, Hampshire

Owner
Steve and Becky Burbidge

Size of Business
1 shop, 19 staff

Type of Bakery
Fourth generation, traditional, family bakery

Steve Burbidge's great-grandfather Harry Bernard Burbidge retired in 1956, handing the bakery over to Charles and Muriel. Charles duly handed the bakery down to his son, John Burbidge in 1963. When John retired, his son Steven took over the reins in 1996 with a mission to return to the bakery's traditional community-style baking roots. On Christmas Eve the bakery roasts turkeys for charity.

'In World War II the US army put in bakery equipment so that we could make bread for the D-Day landing troops', says owner Steve. 'We've only just replaced one of the dough mixers.' The ovens were put in in 1960 and the bakeware stems from the turn of the last century.

The bakery makes all the products on site. Steve and his team bake everything in the shop, working around the clock. Steve describes the bakery's style as traditional English, 'we've got old ovens so we get a good crust'. The bakery sell a range of breads, pastries and cakes, such as rock cakes, Chelsea buns, scones and doughnuts. Their bread selection includes traditional white loaves, 100 percent wholemeal and granary. Steve is proud of his Danish pastries after going to Denmark to learn how to make them, and thinks they're the best in England.

Steve describes the bakery's style as traditional English, 'we've got old ovens so we get a good crust'.

Danish Pastries

MAKES 24

PASTRY

950 g (2 lb 2 oz) strong white bread flour, plus extra for
dusting
50 g (1¾ oz) caster (superfine) sugar
1 teaspoon salt
1 teaspoon ground cardamom
260 g eggs
300 ml (½ pint) water
80 g yeast
35 g (1¼ oz) butter or margarine, plus extra for greasing
400 g (14 oz) margarine

CUSTARD

40 g (1½ oz) dry custard powder
100 ml (3½ fl oz) cold water
300 g (11 oz) ground almonds (almond meal)
300 g (11 oz) margarine
500 g (1 lb 2 oz) chocolate chips
2 eggs, beaten, for the egg wash

CHOCOLATE TOPPING

50 g (1¾ oz) chocolate chips
300 g (11 oz) icing sugar
50 ml (2 fl oz) water
20 g (¾ oz) unsweetened cocoa powder
Small jar apricot jam, for glazing

PASTRY

To make the pastry, put the flour, sugar, salt and cardamom in a large freezerproof container and freeze for 48 hours.
Chill the eggs and water for 48 hours.

Put the eggs and water in the bowl of an electric mixer and whisk in the yeast. Remove the whisk and fit a dough hook. Add the frozen dry ingredients, the 35 g (1¼ oz) butter or margarine and mix for 4 minutes on slow speed. Then turn out onto a floured surface and leave to rest for 20 minutes.

Roll out the dough to 10 mm (³/₈ in) thick. Add the remaining margarine in a block to the centre. Fold the dough around the fat so that it encloses it. Roll out again to 10 mm (³/₈ in), and turn 90 degrees clockwise. Folding from one end turn one-third of the dough over the centre third and do the same with the remaining end. Roll out again to 10 mm (³/₈ in) thick, and turn 90 degrees clockwise. Fold as before. Repeat the rolling and folding once more. Roll out into a rectangle about 3 mm (¹/₈ in) thick.

CUSTARD

To make the custard, mix together all the ingredients in a bowl. Spread the custard mix over the whole length of the dough. Scatter the chocolate chips on top. Roll up the dough into a long sausage and cut slices about 10 mm (³/₈ in) thick. Glaze with egg wash and set aside to prove for 30 minutes. Meanwhile, preheat the oven to 180°C/350°F/Gas mark 4. Arrange the pastries on greased baking sheets and bake for 15 minutes.

CHOCOLATE TOPPING

To make the chocolate topping, mix the ingredients together. Use to part-fill a piping bag. Set aside. Warm the apricot jam with a small amount of water until melted, in a pan over gentle heat. When the pastries come out of the oven, brush with the apricot jam glaze. Pipe the chocolate topping on to the swirls.

Caracoli, Alresford, Hampshire

Owners/Bakers
James and Gail Nichols (mother and son),
Mark Treasure (Executive Chef) and Debbie Hicks
(Sous Chef)

Size of Business
4 shops, 30 staff

Type of Bakery
High end, quirky food store and café

Caracoli, the bakery named after a highly prized coffee bean, bake and supply cakes and savoury food for their own stores in Alresford in Hampshire, Winchester, Guildford and Farnham.

Mum Gail was struck by the stylish, contemporary cafés she found on her travels abroad, which offered amazing coffee, cakes and light lunches while simultaneously incorporating a food store. On returning to the UK she decided to bring this concept to the provinces. The first store opened in the Georgian market town of Alresford, Hampshire, in November 2005.

Mark and Debbie, the bakery team, work from their kitchen on site. The menu changes daily. Their recipes are 'long-time favourites, inspired by international travel and foodie magazines and cook books. We do a lot of experimental baking before going ahead with a new product,' they say. They pride themselves on their 'imaginative and artisan products, which use great quality and fresh ingredients, sourced locally wherever possible.' Best-selling products include chocolate biscuit cake, chocolate brownies, hummingbird cake, chocolate cookies, passionfruit and orange gluten-free cake, banana loaf and Bakewell tarts. Their signature product is their Caracoli muffin and their bestseller is carrot cake.

The Telegraph magazine awarded them Best for Food in the Best Small Shops in Britain, in 2012. They have also won a number of gold stars at the Great Taste awards, the ultimate accolade for fine food, including 2 stars for their chocolate fondant cake and 2 gold stars for banana loaf and triple ginger cake, 1 star for their almond and pistachio cake, passionfruit and orange cake, Caracoli cookie, granola bar, granola, mincemeat, sweet and spicy nuts and Hampshire Ale Cake.

Best-selling products include chocolate biscuit cake, chocolate brownies, hummingbird cake, chocolate cookies, passionfruit and orange gluten-free cake.

Pecorino Cheese, Leek and Chorizo tartlet

MAKES 4–6

PASTRY

400 g (14 oz) plain (all-purpose) flour, plus extra for dusting
200 g (7 oz) butter, chilled and diced
Pinch of salt
1 large egg
100–150 ml (3½–5 fl oz) water

FILLING

1 leek, sliced
1 tablespoon butter
30 g (1 oz) chorizo sausage, thinly sliced
200 g (7 oz) pecorino cheese, grated (shredded)
Sunflower seeds or onion seeds (optional)

SAVOURY CUSTARD

4 eggs
570 ml (19 fl oz) double (heavy) cream
Salt and pepper, to taste

PASTRY

Combine the flour, butter and salt in a large bowl and mix together. Add the egg, then pour in the water a little at a time and mix together until just combined into a pastry. Chill for 1 hour.

Preheat the oven to 160°C/325°F/Gas mark 3. Roll out the pastry on a lightly floured surface to 3 mm (1/8 in) thick, and use to line 4–6 mini tart tins (pans), each 10–12.5 cm (4–5 in) diameter. Line with baking paper and baking beans and bake blind for 20 minutes. Remove from the oven, discard the baking beans and paper and leave to cool. Reduce the oven temperature to 150°/300°F/Gas mark 2.

FILLING

Meanwhile, to make the filling, fry the leek in butter in a frying pan set over low heat until very soft (but with no colour), about 3–4 minutes. Divide between the pastry cases. Fry the chorizo in the same pan until browned on each side.

SAVOURY CUSTARD

To make the custard, in a bowl, whisk the eggs and cream together. Season with salt and pepper.

Fill the pastry cases with the leeks, chorizo, cheese and seeds, if using. Pour the savoury custard over the top. Bake until set, about 15–20 minutes.

Dolcipani Italian Bakery, Devizes, Wiltshire

Owner
Gianni Campanella and sister Sandra Campanella

Type of Bakery
Small Sicilian family bakery producing southern Italian breads, pastries, cakes, tarts and savoury specialities

Size of Business
1 shop, 3 staff

Gianni and his sister Sandra are from a little town called Raddusa, known as 'bread city' on the island of Sicily. He first came to the UK to work in 1977, but returned to Italy to do national service. The siblings opened the Devizes bakery in 1993, following the establishment of their restaurant Isola Bella in the town. 'I trained under Mario Musoni, one of the best chefs in Northern Italy. I was blessed,' says Gianni.

Gianni thinks his natural flare for baking is in his DNA. 'My grandmother made the best bread I ever tasted. We still make it to the same recipe,' he says. In fact, the majority of his recipes, some of which are more than 100 years old, have been passed through the family. He always tries to add a Sicilian twist to everything he bakes.

All produce sold in Dolcipani is baked in the shop and Gianni is extremely proud that the majority of his produce is made by hand. What sets this bakery apart from others is Gianni's 'real' bread. He says that he's infuriated that bakers call their products 'artisan' when it isn't always the case. 'Bread is bread. It's not a miracle,' he says. 'I come from a rural family and Sicilian bread is well known. Bread is part of every Italian family. Without bread you don't eat. There must be bread and wine on the table. We sit down and sort out problems over food. Our breads tend to be more substantial than a lot of the bakery products in speciality shops. I have to have bite to bread. I have to have substance. Most supermarkets and bakeries have the idea that everything has to be light… I know as a baker that the lighter the product, the more chemicals have been added.'

The bakery sells brioche, plain, chocolate and almond Sicilian croissants, biscotti, Sicilian breads called vastedda, with various fillings, pizzas and focaccias.

'Bread is really part of every Italian family.'

Napoli Bread

MAKES 3 LOAVES

500 g (1 lb 2 oz) strong white bread flour, plus extra for
dusting

500 g (1 lb 2 oz) extra strong Manitoba white flour

500 g (1 lb 2 oz) double-milled strong semolina flour, plus
extra for dusting

10 g (¹/₃ oz) fresh yeast

1 litre and 50 ml (1 pint and 17 fl oz) cold water

35 g (1¼ oz) salt, plus extra for serving

35 ml (1¼ fl oz) olive oil, plus extra for greasing and serving

375 g (13 oz) previous day's dough, which you will have
saved in a jar in the refrigerator

oregano, for serving

Sieve the three flours together into the bowl of a food processor fitted with a dough hook and mix well. Add the yeast to the water and mix together until the yeast is dissolved. Add the yeast water to the flour reserving a third of the liquid. NB If you're making bread for the first time, add all of the yeast. If you are making bread for the second or more times reduce the amount of yeast you use. Start the mixer on slow speed and mix until all the water has been absorbed. Add the remaining water and increase the speed to medium. Mix for about 15 minutes.

Add the previous day's dough, if using, small chunks at a time. The more loaves you make, the less yeast you will need since yesterday's dough will provide the ferment. When it has been absorbed, add the salt and olive oil. By now you will hear the noise of the air trapped by the gluten structure of the dough, and it will have a silky appearance. Grease a plastic bowl. Put your dough in it and fold it 4 times as if it were a handkerchief. Turn the dough upside down and cover with a humid cloth. Leave to ferment in a cool place. After 3–5 hours it will have tripled in volume.

Preheat the oven to its hottest setting and add a baking stone if you have one. Liberally dust the work surface with semolina flour. Tip the dough onto the floured surface – it will look very wet. Dust the top with white flour and let rest for 10 minutes. Divide and shape the dough into three equal pieces and place on a baking sheet. Spray the inside of the hot oven with water, add the bread and bake for 15 minutes, then reduce the oven temperature to 210°C/410°F/ Gas mark 6½ and bake for a another 20 minutes. Tap the underside of the bread and if it sounds hollow it is ready. Leave to cool in wicker baskets. Serve slightly warm, sprinkled with olive oil, salt and oregano.

Tip: Sourdough is exactly what it says on the tin — dough gone sour. In order to achieve this you need: long fermentations, good quality strong flours, high water content, common sense and patience. This is the way bread was made in the old days, when modern types of yeast were not available. They used a piece of dough from the previous bake, which by then had gone sour, the more bread you make the stronger the dough is.

Cornfield Bakery, Wheatley, Oxford

Owner/Bakers
Joseph and Brandon Coleman, brothers

Type of Bakery
Traditional family bakery selling a wide range of
breads, couture cakes, traybakes, cupcakes
and pastries

Size of Business
2 shops, 1 industrial unit kitchen, 30 staff

Siblings Joseph and Brandon are the third generation of their family to take ownership of the Cornfield Bakery in Wheatley. Their father Geoff learnt his skills from his father Derek and has passed on all he knows to his sons. Despite that, Joseph is always trying to teach Geoff new baking methods.

All three can remember standing on the same stool in the bakery in their formative years helping their fathers to bake. 'Baking is in the Coleman's blood, it's what we do, it's what we live for,' says Geoff. Geoff's extremely proud of the fact that he's one of the last remaining family bakers in Oxfordshire. Their whole family works in the bakery including a nephew and cousin, wives and daughters.

The business sells 60 percent of its produce wholesale and the balance through retail craft bakers. They make a huge range of traditional bread and cakes including, a range of sourdoughs, speciality flavoured and seeded breads, and more regular loaves. The bakers can turn their hands to all types of baking from bespoke celebration cakes to everyday crusty bread rolls.

Since the business was established in 1972 this bakery has steadily grown to include a shop in nearby Thame. Geoff runs bread-making courses tailoring them for beginners who would like to start making their own bread, to more experienced bakers who would like to refresh or learn new skills.

The bakery still uses Geoff's father's recipes for dough cake (a sweet cake made from white bread dough), a regional bake. Their lardy cake is the next bestseller.

'Baking is in the Coleman's blood, it's what we do, it's what we live for.'

Lardy Cake

MAKES 8

DOUGH

1 kg (2¼ lb) strong white bread flour, plus extra for dusting
19 g (¾ oz) salt
60 g (2 oz) brown sugar
13 g (½ oz) bread improver
100 g (3½ oz) margarine
30 g (1 oz) yeast
375 ml (13 fl oz) warm water
120 ml (4 fl oz) milk
60 g egg, beaten (about 1 medium–large egg)

FILLING

375 g (13 oz) lard
290 g (10¼ oz) demerara (raw) sugar
150 g (5 oz) currants
150 g (5 oz) sultanas (golden raisins)

TOPPING

60 g (2 oz) golden (light corn) syrup
60 g (2 oz) mixed dried fruit

DOUGH

In a large bowl, mix together the flour, salt, sugar and bread improver. Add the margarine, yeast, warm water, milk and beaten egg and mix until it comes together as a dough. Turn out onto a lightly floured surface and knead until smooth and soft. Put it in a bowl, cover and set aside to rest in a warm place for 30 minutes.

FILLING

Meanwhile, mix all the filling ingredients together. Roll out the dough into a rectangle, on a lightly floured surface. Spread the filling over two-thirds of the dough and turn the dough 90 degrees and fold in half. Rest for 5 minutes. Roll the dough into a rectangle and half turn again. Rest for 5 minutes. Roll the dough into a rectangle. Cut into 8 even squares.

TOPPING

Grease and line eight 15 cm (6 in) round tins (pans) with baking paper. Drizzle golden syrup into each tin followed by the mixed fruit. Mould the dough pieces into a round shape and place into the tins. Cover and leave to prove for 30 minutes in a warm place.

Meanwhile, preheat the oven to 200°C/400°F/Gas mark 6. Bake for approximately 30 minutes. Leave to rest in the tin for 10 minutes, then turn out on to a wire rack to go cold.

The Sandwich Box, Cheltenham

· ·

Owner
Dominic and mum, Annette Salter

Type of Bakery
Quirky, artisan bakery takeaway selling breads,
sandwiches, pastries, traybakes and cakes

Size of Business
1 shop, 3 staff

A passion for foraging for free food and success at allotment gardening have proved to be handy skills for the owners of The Sandwich Box, mother and son team Dominic and Annette. Dom's dad saw the business advertised nine years ago after he was made redundant, but a new job offer meant that he passed on the business opportunity to his wife and son. The business has been established for 40 years and originally it was supplied with bread, but Dom thought he could do better and now most of the produce is baked on site. He now considers himself to be 'the ultimate bread man'. Bread has become something of an obsession for Dom and he admits he's most happy when making his long fermented sourdough. He learnt his skills from catering college as well as courses at Shipton Mill and E5 Bakehouse, then continued to develop his breads though experimentation. Dominic says 'this has been my life since the age of 18. It really is all I've ever known.'

Everything this duo make is either sourced locally, from an allotment or from foraging. Dominic's love of foraging stems from his childhood and he now takes his children out to forage for exciting ingredients. He always chooses new, interesting flavours in his breads; nettle bread being his favourite at the moment.

Annette has baked all of her life as a hobby. She now grows some of their produce in her allotment and makes some of the cakes and traybakes. Their ethos is all about being fresh and rustic.

Dom's success has continued with him winning an award at the World Bread Awards 2013 with his Cheltenham muesli and marmalade breakfast loaf.

Dominic's love of foraging stems from his childhood and he now takes his children out to forage for exciting ingredients.

Nettle and Roast Onion Loaf

MAKES 2 LOAVES

400 g (14 oz) strong white bread flour, plus extra for dusting
50 g (1¾ oz) rye flour
50 g (1¾ oz) spelt flour
1 teaspoon nettles, dried and ground
2 teaspoons salt
Pinch of hemp seeds, toasted

300 ml (½ pint) stinging nettle beer or real ale
200 g (7 oz) sourdough starter (see Before You Begin)
Dash of rapeseed oil
2 small red onions, chopped and roasted in olive oil, until soft
and left to cool

Fit a dough hook attachment to an electric mixer. Combine the flours, nettles and salt in the mixer bowl. Add the hemp seeds, beer, and rapeseed oil and mix for 7 minutes. Add the roasted red onions and mix for 1 minute. Turn out the dough onto a floured surface and flatten it into a rectangle. Bring the top third over the centre third and the bottom third over the top and bring back to a ball. This is called a bench turn and encourages yeast growth. Leave to rise for 1 hour in a sealed container at room at room temperature. Make a bench turn as before and leave rise again for 1 hour. Repeat this process one more time.

Divide into two equal amounts and shape into 2 loaves and prove for 2–5 hours. (If you have a warm room it may take 2 hours to double in size but if you have a cold room it may take 5 hours.)

Preheat the oven to 240°C/475°F/Gas mark 9 and place a baking tray in the base of the oven. As you put the loaves in to bake, pour a cup of water into the baking tray to create steam. Bake for 30 minutes, or until golden brown. The underside will sound hollow when tapped.

Gatineau, Summertown, Oxford

Owner
Hervé Gatineau

Size of Business
1 shop, 8 staff

Type of Bakery
French pâtisserie selling cakes, pastries and bread

Situated in the upmarket Summertown area of Oxford, Gatineau pâtisserie offers a little piece of French culture in this old city. Baker Hervé, makes the finest artisan produce in the French / European pâtisserie and boulangerie tradition: premium cakes, pastries, savouries and bread – all made with the highest quality ingredients, creative flair, taste combinations and attention to detail.

Hervé set up the pâtisserie in Oxford in 2007, his first solo enterprise after working as head of pastry at Maison Blanc in London's Park Royal. After training in Toulouse as an apprentice aged 15, Hervé Gatineau worked as a pastry chef in businesses abroad, including the renowned Laurent Bakery in Sydney, Australia, where he learned a variety of new skills and techniques.

He continually strives to improve his recipes, always working with quality ingredients, focusing on taste and using his artistic skills to create beautiful products. A perfectionist, Hervé likes to push the boundaries and try new things. He also keeps in touch with the latest European trends in pâtisserie and visits France annually to work with current leaders in pastry.

All pâtisserie and viennoiserie are made on site. The bakery also makes a range of bread and baguettes. Jams and honeys are imported from France.

A perfectionist, Hervé likes to push the boundaries and try new things.

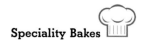

Croquant Valrhona

MAKES 1 CAKE

PRALINE CROQUANT
75 g (2½ oz) white chocolate
425 g (15 oz) praline paste
200 g (7 oz) cornflakes

GANACHE MOUSSE
6 g ($^1/_8$ oz) gelatine leaves
200 g (7 oz) single (light) cream
225 g (8 oz) good quality milk chocolate, broken into chunks
400 g (14 oz) double (heavy) cream

MILK CHOCOLATE PRALINE GLAZE
250 ml (9 fl oz) water
10 g ($^1/_3$ oz) jam pectine
65 g (2¼ oz) caster sugar
200 g (7 oz) caster (superfine) sugar
15 g (½ oz) liquid inverted glucose
50 g (1¾ oz) milk chocolate
50 g (1¾ oz) praline paste

PRALINE CROQUANT
Melt the white chocolate in a bowl set over a pan of gently simmering water. Add the praline paste. Stir both ingredients with a rubber spatula. Add the cornflakes to the mix. Stir well again. Pour the mix into a 20 cm (8 in) flexi mould. Refrigerate while you make the mousse mix.

GANACHE MOUSSE
Soak the gelatine leaves in cold water, following the manufacturer's instructions. In a small pan heat the single cream to 50°C. Squeeze the gelatine leaves in your hands, then add it to the heated cream. Add the chocolate to the cream. Mix with a spatula until smooth.

Whip the double cream until thick. Pour the ganache into the thickened whipped cream, then fold both together with a rubber spatula until smooth. Pour onto the crunchy praline base. Smooth the mousse with a palette knife. Freeze for 3 hours minimum.

MILK CHOCOLATE PRALINE GLAZE
Heat the water in a pan to 50°C. In a bowl mix the pectine with the caster sugar. Add the sugar and pectin mix to the water slowly using a whisk. Whisk vigorously over medium heat for 1 minute. Remove from the heat and add the 200 g (7 oz) of caster sugar and glucose to the mix. Add the chocolate and praline paste to the pan. Using a hand blender, stir the mix for one minute. Cover with cling film (plastic wrap) and refrigerate until cooled down.

Take the cake out of the freezer. Bring the glaze to 27°C and pour over the mousse and spread evenly

East and West Bakery, Barnstaple, Devon

Owner
Graham and Claire Principe

Type of Bakery
Traditional family bakery and pâtisserie

Size of Business
1 shop, 15 staff

East and West Bakery has been trading for 16 years on the oldest street in Barnstaple. Owner Graham bought the business in 1997 and started by making breads and cakes that customers requested. Graham worked as a baker's apprentice for four years after he left school, and then worked in a Jewish bakery making bagels and bloomers. Then, in 1969, he joined the merchant navy as a baker and travelled the world. In-between times he worked as a pastry chef including a spell at Brighton's Grand Hotel, and backpacked around the world. He named his bakery East and West after his travels.

When he married, he travelled the world for two years with his wife. Before owning the bakery they ran a restaurant together for 12 years.

Graham has found the recipes he uses in an assortment of places including very old and modern cookbooks, on the internet, from travels, friends and other bakeries he has worked in. They include many West Country favourites in their repertoire. Graham caters for coeliacs and makes a large selection of gluten-free products, including nine different varieties of sponges, four types of roulade, two different meringues, and a fabulous ganache mousse. The low GI bread is their biggest seller.

'I'm passionate about my business. I love life and I love baking. I'm very, very proud of what we do', he says. 'I'm a big believer in training and the future of the baking world – I want to give a little bit back.'

'I'm a big believer in training and the future of the baking world – I want to give a little bit back.'

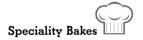

Rum Baba

MAKES 9

DOUGH

250 g (9 oz) strong white bread flour

1 teaspoon caster (superfine) sugar

½ teaspoon salt

3 eggs

20 g (¾ oz) fresh yeast

40 ml (1¼ fl oz) tepid milk

190 g (6½ oz) butter

100 g (3½ oz) sultanas (golden raisins)

100 g (3½ oz) currants

SYRUP

500 ml (17 fl oz) boiling water

250 g (9 oz) caster (superfine) sugar

Zest and juice of 2 lemons

Zest and juice of 2 oranges

½ teaspoon vanilla extract

½ teaspoon lemon extract

9 teaspoons rum

500 g (1 lb 2 oz) apricot jam, to glaze

DOUGH

To make the dough, pour the flour, sugar and salt into the bowl of an electric mixer and mix together. Break the eggs directly into the bowl.

Dissolve the yeast in the milk in a small bowl. Start to mix the flour and sugar mixture on slow speed and drizzle the yeast and milk mixture in slowly. Mix on a high speed for 7 minutes. The dough needs to have a stringy consistency. Leave to prove for 15–20 minutes, until it rises.

Add the butter and beat on a high speed for 2 minutes. Leave to rest for 5 minutes before adding the dried fruit and mix by hand just enough to combine. Weigh out 9 equal portions and place into greased brioche tins (pans). Prove in a warm place for 10 minutes, until doubled in size. Preheat the oven to 220°C/425°F/Gas mark 7. Bake for 13–15 minutes.

SYRUP

To make the syrup, pour 1 litre (1¾ pints) of boiling water into a pan. Add the sugar and set over medium heat until boiling. Whisk the mixture until it dissolves to a syrup. Remove from the heat and leave to cool for 3–4 minutes, then add the zest and juice of the oranges and lemons, lemon and vanilla extracts. Decant into a large baking dish. Place the baked babas in the syrup and leave to soak. Turn the babas over to soak the other side in syrup and leave in the refrigerator overnight so that the syrup is completely absorbed. Pour the rum over the babas. Remove from the dish and leave to dry. Heat the apricot jam in a pan over medium heat and bring to the boil. Using a pastry brush, glaze the babas with the boiled jam to seal in the flavours and give them a golden brown colour.

Seeds 2 Bakery, Totnes, Devon

Owners
Darren Thorne and Mike Ashton

Type of Bakery
Vegetarian artisan bakery selling breads, cakes,
traybakes and pastries

Size of Business
1 shop, 2 staff

Seeds 2 Bakery began life as a health food shop more than 30 years ago. Owner Darren turned it into a bakery serving rustic, local, hand-crafted baked goods, when he took hold of the reins three years ago. Both Darren and Mike are self-taught and are passionate about their products and love creating original tastes using local and seasonal ingredients. This independent bakery makes rustic bread, cakes and pastries fusing only natural ingredients and incorporating as much local and seasonal produce as possible. The shop is well established and still growing in popularity. Totnes has a very food-conscious community who are keen to buy quality local food.

Darren admits to being 'slightly obsessed' with bread. He's extremely experimental and is always trying to improve his products. He likes to infuse natural colours, and flavours into his products, making them vibrant in colour and taste. His favourite breads are apple and beetroot, which is bright pink, and fennel and spinach, which is bright green.

Mike has been a baker all his life, while Darren was a plumber by training. He hopes his youngest son will take over the business in the near future.

Both men are enthusiastic experimental bakers and the vast majority of their recipes are adaptations from their travels.

They are both extremely experimental bakers with the vast majority of their recipes being adaptations from their travels.

Spinach and Fennel Bread

MAKES 2 LOAVES

BREAD DOUGH
600 g (1 lb 6 oz) stoneground white flour
8 g (¼ oz) sea salt
350 ml (12 fl oz) warm water
200 g (7 oz) fresh spinach
6 g (¼ oz) fennel seeds
150 g (5 oz) ferment

FERMENT
100 ml (3½ fl oz) water
50 g (1¾ oz) strong white bread flour
4 g live yeast

FERMENT
To make the ferment, mix the ingredients together in a large bowl, cover and leave for at least 24 hours at room temperature.

BREAD DOUGH
Put the flour, salt, water, ferment and yeast in the bowl of an electric mixer and mix on a slow speed.

Meanwhile, put the spinach in a food processor and blend to a rough paste. Add the fennel seeds and blend for 5 seconds (to crack them). Add the paste to the dough mixture and mix for 6–7 minutes on low speed. Leave to rest for 10 minutes. Beat on medium speed for 15 minutes. Tip out of the mixer bowl into an oiled bowl, turn twice and leave for 45–60 minutes, then turn again.

Leave again for 45–60 minutes, then turn again to develop the taste and texture of the bread. Repeat once more. Divide into 2 portions and loosely shape the loaves, taking care not to squash them. Set aside to rest for 10 minutes. Preheat the oven to 240°C/475°F/Gas mark 9. Reshape the loaves and place on baking sheets leave to rise for 15–20 minutes. Dust with flour and make a single slash with a sharp knife 1 cm (³/₈ in) as desired. Spray the hot oven with water as you add the bread and bake for 35–45 minutes.

The Cottage Kitchen, Kingsbridge, Devon

Owner/Baker
Nicola Barlow (Owner) and Philip Cooling (Pastry Chef)

Size of Business
1 shop, 1 off-site unit, 8 staff

Type of Bakery
Couture cakes, traybakes, cupcakes, pastries

The Cottage Kitchen makes and sells traditional cakes (like granny used to make) as well as traybakes, cupcakes and pastries. The business was started 18 years ago by Nicola, who baked from her home kitchen to begin with. The business now has a dedicated shop in town.

Philip joined the business a couple of years ago. They can both turn their hands to all types of baking and although they don't bake bread to sell they're both as capable of making bread as 'the baker next door'. They pride themselves on using those traditional methods of baking, a world away from mass production. All the produce used in the baking is sourced locally and made in the off-site unit.

Nicola's range of cakes is highly respected locally and she's extremely proud of her business and what she's achieved.

The Cottage Kitchen have won 26 awards over the past 8 years: in 2011, 6 'Taste of The West' Awards, including Gold for their millionaire slice and 5 bronze awards for their apple and cinnamon cake, lemon tart, steak pasty, gluten-free Victoria sandwich and spiced carrot cake. In October 2011 they also won a Gold one star Great Taste Award from The Guild of Fine Food for their gluten-free carrot cake. They currently hold 26 awards, all won over the last five years, for their delicious cakes and tarts.

The Cottage Kitchen have won 26 awards over the past 8 years

Spiced Carrot Cake

MAKES 1 CAKE

SPONGE
280 g (10 oz) self-raising (self-rising) flour
2 teaspoons ground ginger
2 teaspoons ground cinnamon
2 teaspoons baking powder
350 g (12 oz) caster (superfine) sugar
4 eggs
280 ml (9 fl oz) sunflower oil, plus extra for greasing
280 g (10 oz) carrots, grated (shredded)
90 g (3½ oz) walnuts, chopped

TOPPING
70 g (2¼ oz) butter, softened
200 g (7 oz) cream cheese, softened
400 g (14 oz) icing (confectioners') sugar, sifted
½ teaspoon cinnamon
150 g (5 oz) white chocolate curls (see *chocolate and orange cheesecakes*)

Preheat the oven to 150°C/300°F/Gas mark 2. Grease and line a 20 cm (8 in) round cake tin (pan) with baking paper.

SPONGE
Sieve the flour into a large bowl. Add the spices and baking powder. Add the sugar, eggs, oil and grated carrots and beat together using an electric mixer until it changes colour. Don't over-mix otherwise the cake will become too dense. Pour into the prepared tin and bake for 1 hour, or until the top is spongy. Leave to set in the tin for a few minutes before turning out onto a wire rack to cool for 2 hours or more.

TOPPING
To make the topping, put the butter and cream cheese in a large mixing bowl, sift in the icing sugar and cinnamon. Beat until light and smooth. Slice the cooled cake in half and put one half on a serving plate. Spread half the topping over the sponge layer and top with the other layer of sponge.

Part-fill a piping bag with the rest of the topping and use to pipe decoration along the cake edges. Decorate with walnuts and white chocolate curls.

Afternoon Tea

Few things are more quintessentisally British than afternoon tea. This 19th-century invention was introduced to stave off hunger in the later afternoon, but soon became a vehicle to show off exquisite porcelain, good manners and the food of a fine cook. Dainty sandwiches, sweet and savoury pastries, morsels of rich, sweet cake, and jam and cream filled scones, all beautifully presented, are prerequisite for this meal. For judge Mich Turner the bakes in this chapter, showcase a wonderful selection of Afternoon Tea recipes. They are all about being creative and innovative.

BIRDHOUSE BAKERY

Meringues

MAKES 12–14

MERINGUES
4 egg whites
225 g (8 oz) caster (superfine) sugar, plus extra for dusting

FILLING
28 strawberry halves, to serve
250 ml (8 fl oz) whipped cream, to serve

Preheat the oven to 110°C/225°F/Gas mark ¼.

MERINGUES
Whisk the egg whites in a clean, grease-free bowl, until very stiff. Add the sugar a tablespoon at a time whisking as you go until all the sugar has been incorporated. Spoon or pipe the meringues onto a baking sheet lined with baking paper. Dust a little sugar over the top, then bake for 2 hours, switch off the oven but leave the meringues in the oven to cool.

FILLING
Serve with strawberries and cream.

Tip: Swirl some raspberry jam through the meringue mixture to get a multi-coloured meringue, if you like.

Chocolate Orange and Whisky tarts

MAKES 12–14

SWEET PASTRY
225 g (8 oz) plain (all-purpose) flour, plus extra for dusting
115 g (4 oz) butter
30 g (1 oz) sugar
2 egg yolks
Cold water
1 small egg, for the egg wash

GANACHE FILLING
225 g (8 oz) whiskey and bitter orange marmalade
200 ml (7 fl oz) double (heavy) cream
50 g (1¾ oz) butter
300 g (11 oz) dark (bittersweet) chocolate
Zest of 1 orange and juice of ½ orange,
    plus extra zest for decorating

SWEET PASTRY
To make the pastry, in a large bowl, rub the flour and butter together with your fingertips until the mixture resembles fine breadcrumbs. Stir through the sugar, then add the egg yolks and beat until combined. Add a drizzle of cold water to bring the mixture together. Wrap in cling film (plastic wrap) and refrigerate to chill.

Preheat the oven to 180°C/350°F/Gas mark 4. Roll out on a lightly floured surface to a depth of 3 mm ($^1/_8$ in) and use to line the base and sides of 12 tins each 39 cm (3½ in) diameter. Add a layer of baking paper to each and fill with baking beans. Bake for 10 minutes. Remove the baking beans and paper and return to the oven for another 5 minutes. Remove from the oven, brush with egg wash and return to the oven for 2 more minutes, then turn out onto a wire rack and leave to cool completely.

GANACHE FILLING
Spread 1 tablespoon of the whiskey marmalade over the base of the pastry case.

To make the ganache, heat the cream in a heavy saucepan until just boiling. Remove from the heat and add the butter and chocolate. Stir slowly and mix thoroughly until both have melted and the ganache is silky smooth. Add the orange zest and mix through.

Gently pour the chocolate mixture into the tartlet cases and leave to set for at least 1 hour in a cool place. Decorate with a twist of orange zest.

Scones with Homemade Jam and Cream

APPLEBY BAKERY

MAKES 9

SCONES

450 g (1 lb) self-raising (self-rising) flour, plus extra for dusting
90 g (3 oz) sugar
125 g (4½ oz) margarine
2 eggs, beaten
milk, to mix

JAM (JELLY)

450 g (1 lb) raspberries
450 g (1 lb) sugar
3 oz (85 g) butter
Clotted cream, to serve

Preheat the oven to 180°C/350°F/Gas mark 4.

SCONES

To make the scones, in a bowl, mix together the flour and sugar. Add the margarine and rub together with your fingertips until the mixture resembles fine breadcrumbs. Make a well in the centre, add the eggs and mix together. Add a little milk at a time and mix together until the mixture comes together. Tip out onto a lightly floured surface, knead a little to mix together into a ball. Flatten with the heel of your hand until it is the same depth as the cookie cutter. Stamp out scones and place on a baking sheet lined with baking paper. Bake for 15 minutes, or until golden.

JAM

Meanwhile, to make the jam, put the raspberries in a heavy-based pan, place over medium heat and bring to the boil. Pour the sugar into a baking tray, shake to even out and place in the oven to warm for a few minutes while the scones bake. Add the warm sugar to the raspberries and simmer for 10 minutes. Add the butter and stir in. Leave to cool.

Serve the scones topped with jam and cream.

Sausage Rolls

MAKES 6 LARGE ROLLS

PASTRY

225 g (8 oz) plain (all-purpose) flour, plus extra for dusting
Pinch salt
150 g (5 oz) lard and margarine mixed
150 ml (¼ pint) cold water
milk, to seal

FILLING

225 g (8 oz) coarse Cumberland sausagemeat
salt and pepper, to taste

Preheat the oven to 180°C/350°C/Gas mark 4. Lightly grease a baking sheet.

PASTRY

To make the pastry, put the flour and salt into a large mixing bowl. Rub in the lard or margarine with your fingertips until the mixture resembles fine breadcrumbs. Add just enough water, a little at a time, to bring the mixture together. Turn out onto a lightly floured surface and knead lightly, then roll out to a rectangle and to 3 mm ($^1/_8$ in) thick. Cut into three strips.

FILLING

Arrange the sausagemeat evenly down the centre of the three pastry strips. Season with salt and pepper, then fold the pastry over to encase the sausagemeat. Seal the edges with a little milk. Cut each in half. Brush the outer casing with milk.

Bake on the prepared baking sheet for about 20 minutes. Turn them once while they are cooking so that the undersides are cooked.

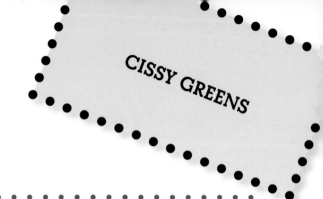
CISSY GREENS

Manchester Muffins

MAKES 12

SPONGE

325 g (12 oz) self-raising (self-rising) flour
Pinch of salt
1½ teaspoons baking powder
175 g (6 oz) caster (superfine) sugar
3 eggs
5–6 tablespoons milk
280 g (10 oz) glacé cherries very finely chopped
100 g (3½ oz) desiccated (dry unsweetened shredded)
    coconut

TOPPING

200 g (7 oz) instant custard powder
60 ml (2¼ fl oz) water
12 teaspoons apple and raspberry jam
1 banana, finely diced
3 glacé cherries, cut into quarters
30 g (1 oz) desiccated (dry unsweetened shredded) coconut

Preheat the oven to 200°C/400°F/Gas mark 6. Line the cups of a muffin tray with paper cases.

SPONGE

Sift the flour, salt, baking powder and sugar together into a large bowl. In a small bowl, beat the eggs, milk and oil together, then add to flour mixture. Using electric beaters, mix on second speed for 4 minutes. Add the coconut and chopped cherries. Divide the batter between the paper cases and bake for 20–25 minutes. Leave to cool on a wire rack. When cold, core out the centre of the muffins.

TOPPING

Make the custard by mixing the custard powder with the water following the manufacturer's instructions. It should be thick. Cut out a core from each muffin, fill with jam, diced banana, top with cold custard, a cherry quarter and a sprinkling of coconut.

Deconstructed Pork Pie

MAKES 4–5

PASTRY

150 g (5 oz) white fat
450 g (1 lb) plain (all-purpose) flour, plus extra for dusting
½ teaspoon salt
4 tablespoons milk
150 ml (5 fl oz) water
1 egg, beaten, to glaze

FILLING

325 g (12 oz) coarse Cumberland sausagemeat
Salt and pepper, to season
Roast peppers to decorate,

PASTRY

In a large bowl, rub the white fat into the flour and salt using your fingertips until the mixture resembles fine breadcrumbs. Stir in the milk and just enough water to mix to a smooth paste. Cover and leave to rest for 20 minutes. Preheat the oven to 200°C/400°F/Gas mark 6. Grease and line a baking sheet.

On a lightly floured surface, roll out the pastry to 3 mm ($^1/_8$ in) thickness and stamp out rounds. Place on the baking sheet. Brush with egg wash, then make a hole in the centre of each using a cocktail stick. Bake for 15 minutes, or until golden.

FILLING

Meanwhile, put the sausagemeat on a baking tray and roll out to 7 mm ($^1/_3$ in thick). Season to taste. Bake in the oven with the pastry. Remove from the oven and when cool enough to handle, stamp out rounds the same size as the pastry. Stack a sausagemeat round on a pastry round, then stack a second pastry and sausagemeat round on too of another. Finish the stack with a pastry round and hold each together with a cocktail stick. Top with a slice of roasted pepper.

COWBURNS

Raspberry Roulade

MAKES 1 ROULADE

SPONGE
6 eggs, separated
200 g (7 oz) caster (superfine) sugar, plus extra for sprinkling
Zest of 1 lemon
150 g (5 oz) potato flour

FILLING
500 ml (17 fl oz) whipping cream
Sugar, to taste
50 ml (2 fl oz) raspberry liqueur or raspberry syrup
100 g (3½ oz) raspberries drizzled with 2 tablespoons of lemon juice
Icing (confectioners') sugar, for dusting

Preheat the oven to 160°C/325°F/Gas mark 3. Line a baking sheet with silicone paper.

SPONGE
Part-fill a pan with water and place over medium heat. Put the egg yolks, half the sugar, and the lemon zest in a mixing bowl and rest the bowl on the pan of water, but so that the base is not touching the water. The water should simmer gently but not boil. Whisk the ingredients together using electric beaters until pale and the volume has increased, 10–15 minutes, or when the beaters will draw a figure of eight through the batter. Remove from the heat.

In a separate bowl, whisk the egg whites and the rest of the sugar until the mixture forms gentle peaks. Sieve the potato flour into the egg whites and fold in gently using a metal spoon until fully incorporated, without losing volume. In three stages, gently fold the egg white mixture into the egg yolk mixture, trying to retain the volume. Tip the batter onto the prepared baking sheet and bake for 10 minutes, or until springy on top and without colour. Sprinkle with sugar and turn out onto a moist dish towel and allow to cool without taking the paper away.

FILLING
Put the cream and sugar in a bowl and whip until mousse-like. When the sponge is cool, remove the backing paper and soak with raspberry liqueur or syrup. Turn the sponge so that the long edge faces you. Spread a layer of sweetened cream across the bottom one-third and 5 cm (2 in) from the edge. Place the raspberries in a line on top of the cream. With the cloth under the sponge, start to roll up making sure there is even tension. Cut away any excess sponge, roll up tightly and refrigerate. Dust with icing sugar.

Sour Cherry Bakewells

MAKES 8–10

SPONGE

125 g (4½ oz) unsalted butter, softened
125 g (4½ oz) caster (superfine) sugar
2 large eggs, beaten
Pinch of cinnamon
125 g (4½ oz) ground almonds (almond meal)
60 g (2 oz) dried pitted sour cherries

TOPPING

30 g (1 oz) dried pitted sour cherries, finely chopped
75 g (2½ oz) Icing (confectioners') sugar
1 teaspoon lemon juice

Preheat the oven to 160°C/325°F/Gas mark 3. Grease and line a tray of muffin cups.

SPONGE

In a large bowl, beat the butter and sugar until the sugar has dissolved and the mixture is light. Gradually add the beaten egg and the cinnamon until all combined. Add the ground almonds, and stir well. Pour the mixture into a piping bag and use to three-quarters fill the lined muffin patties with batter, placing some cherries in each as you go. Bake for 15–17 minutes. Turn out onto a wire rack to go cold.

TOPPING

Top with the finely chopped cherries. Mix the icing sugar and lemon juice together in a small bowl until it is thick enough to glaze the back of a spoon. Spoon a little on top of each bakewell.

Brioche with Parma Ham and Basil Butter

MAKES 2 LOAVES

BRIOCHE
600 g (1 lb 6 oz) strong white bread flour, plus extra
   for dusting
50 g (1 ¾ oz) sugar
20 g (¾ oz) fresh yeast
1½ teaspoons salt
2 eggs
220 ml (7 fl oz) milk
4 teaspoons sunflower oil
300 g (11 oz) butter

BASIL BUTTER
300 ml (½ pint) double (heavy) cream
pinch salt
4 basil leaves

Parma ham, to fill

BRIOCHE
Put the flour, sugar, yeast and salt in a large bowl ensuring that the salt doesn't come into contact with the yeast. In a separate bowl whisk together the eggs, milk and oil. Add the wet ingredients to the dry ingredients, mix to combine with your hands and bring together to form a dough. Knead on a lightly floured surface for 8–10 minutes gradually incorporating the butter into the dough as you work. Put the dough in an oiled bowl, cover and leave to rise in a draught-free place until doubled in size (about 1½–2½ hours).

Put the dough on a work surface, cut in half, and roll each on a lightly floured surface until you have a 10 cm (4 in) thick sausage shape. Leave to prove again until doubled in size, about 1½–2 hours. Bake at 200°C/400°F/Gas mark 6 for 30 minutes. Leave to set for a few minutes then turn out onto a wire rack to go cold.

BASIL BUTTER
To make the basil butter, whisk the cream in a large bowl until it separates. Remove the butter and discard the liquid. Place the butter in muslin and twist tight until all the buttermilk has drained away. Return to a mixing bowl. Add a pinch of salt to the butter. Finely chop the basil and stir well until incorporated. Chill to set.

To assemble the sandwiches, cut thin slices of brioche, spread with butter and top with slices of Parma ham.

Chocolate Whoopie Pies

MAKES 8

COOKIE DOUGH
110 g (4 oz) self-raising (self-rising) flour
110 g (4 oz) soft brown sugar
30 g (1 oz) unsweetened cocoa powder
¼ teaspoon salt
110 g (4 oz) butter, softened
2 eggs

GANACHE
300 g (11 oz) milk chocolate, broken into chunks
150 ml (¼ pint) whipping cream
Pinch of salt

BUTTERCREAM
80 g (3 oz) butter, softened
160 g (5½ oz) icing (confectioners') sugar
½ teaspoon vanilla extract
Pinch of salt

Preheat the oven to 160°C/325°F/Gas mark 3. Line two baking sheets with baking paper.

COOKIE DOUGH
To make the cookied dough, add all the dry ingredients to the bowl of an electric mixer and mix until combined. Add the butter and eggs and mix until just combined. Spoon 16 dessert spoons of the batter onto the prepared baking sheets, spacing them apart and bake for 10 minutes. Leave to set for a few minutes then turn out on to a wire rack to go cold.

GANACHE
To make the ganache, put the ingredients in a bowl and set it over a pan of gently simmering water. Stir until melted and continue to stir until the mixture forms a thickened sauce.
Remove the bowl from the pan and set aside to cool.

BUTTERCREAM
Meanwhile, make the filling. In a bowl, beat the butter until pale. Add the icing sugar, vanilla and salt and beat until smooth and creamy. Use to part-fill a piping bag fitted with a large nozzle.

To construct the whoopie pies, spread a layer of ganache on the underside of each cookie. Pipe buttercream on top of the ganache on eight of the cookies. Sandwich together.

THE ANGEL'S SHARE

Triple Decker Ham Sandwiches

EACH MAKES 2 LARGE LOAVES

WHITE SODA BREAD

1 kg (2¼ lb) strong white bread flour
40 g (1½ oz) baking powder
80 g (3 oz) sugar
150 g (5 oz) butter, melted, plus extra for greasing
250 g (9 oz) Wensleydale cheese, coarsely grated (shredded), to taste
Salt and pepper, to taste
1 litre (1¾ pints) buttermilk or milk

BROWN SODA BREAD

500 g (1 lb 2 oz) rye flour
500 g (1 lb 2 oz) wholemeal (whole-wheat) flour
40 g (1½ oz) baking powder
80 g (3 oz) sugar
150 g (5 oz) butter
Salt and pepper, to taste

FILLING

125 g (4½ oz) butter
12 large slices of ham
250 g (9 oz) soft cream cheese
Freshly ground black pepper

WHITE SODA BREAD

To make the white soda bread, mix all the dry ingredients together in a large bowl with the seasoning. Add the melted butter, cheese, buttermilk or milk and form a soft dough. Knead together until smooth, approximately 10 minutes. Form into loaves and place in lightly oiled bread tins. Bake for approximately 30 minutes at 220°C/425°F/Gas mark 7. Turn out onto a wire rack to go cold.

BROWN SODA BREAD

Make as for the white soda bread.

FILLING

Thinly slice the loaves and butter one side of each slice. Cover one type of bread with ham and the other type of bread with cream cheese. Put the cream-cheese covered bread on the work surface. Stack the ham covered bread on top. Top with another buttered slice of bread, placing the buttered side down, and alternating the colourways as you work. Trim off the crusts and cut into dainty sandwiches.

Savoury Choux with Whitby Crab

MAKES 8–12

CHOUX PASTRY
120 ml (4 fl oz) milk
120 ml (4 fl oz) water
100 g (3½ oz) butter, diced
Pinch of salt
1 teaspoon caster (superfine) sugar
130 g (4¼ oz) plain (all-purpose) flour, sifted
4 eggs
1 heaped teaspoon each of dill and chervil, chopped
Egg wash, made by mixing 1 egg yolk with 1 tablespoon milk

FILLING
225 g (8 oz) crab meat
85 g (3 oz) mayonnaise
Black pepper, to taste
Lemon juice, to taste
Chervil, to garnish

Preheat the oven to 180°C/350°F/Gas mark 4. Line 2 baking sheets with baking paper.

CHOUX PASTRY
Put the milk, water, butter, salt and sugar in a pan together over low heat. Bring to the boil, then remove from the heat immediately and sift in the flour. Beat until smooth. Return to the heat for 1 minute to dry out the paste.
Beat in the eggs, quickly, one at a time until smooth and shiny. Add the chopped herbs and stir through. Spoon the mixture into a piping bag. Pipe rounds about the size of a large coin, spaced well apart, onto a baking sheet lined with baking paper. Brush each with egg wash and bake for about 15 minutes until the outside is dry and crisp. Leave to cool on a wire rack.

FILLING
To make the filling, in a bowl, mix the crab meat with the mayonnaise, pepper and lemon juice. Split the choux buns in two and fill generously. Garnish with chervil.

Chocolate Brownies

· ·

MAKES 1 TRAY

500 g (1 lb 2 oz) butter
500 g (1 lb 2 oz) caster (superfine) sugar
600 g (1 lb 6 oz) Belgian chocolate chips
350 g (12 oz) plain (all-purpose) flour
5 eggs
3 egg yolks
400 g (14 oz) Lexia raisins soaked in
    Pedro Ximenez sherry for at least 24 hours
Piped chocolate shapes, to decorate

Preheat the oven to 160°C/300°F/Gas mark 3. Line a baking tray with baking paper.

Melt the butter in a saucepan over a gentle heat. Add the sugar and stir until dissolved. Remove from the heat, add the chocolate chips and stir until melted. Beat in the sifted flour, then the eggs and egg yolks. Beat thoroughly to combine. Drain the soaked raisins and stir through the mixture. Pour into the baking tray and bake for 25–30 minutes, until they have a slight wobble. Decorate with piped chocolate shapes, if you like.

Choux Swans with Cream and Strawberries

THE PUDDING ROOM

MAKES 6

CHOUX PASTRY
150 ml (¼ pint) equal parts milk and water mixed
60 g (2 oz) butter
90 g (3 oz) plain (all-purpose) flour
2 eggs

FILLING
250 ml (8 fl oz) double (heavy) cream
1 tablespoon sugar
3 strawberries, to decorate

Preheat the oven to 190°C/375°F/Gas mark 5.

CHOUX PASTRY

To make the choux pastry, put the milk and water mixture and butter in a saucepan and set over high heat. Bring to a rapid boil. Remove from the heat. Add the flour and beat hard with a wooden spoon until the mixture leaves the sides of the saucepan. Tip into a mixing bowl, add the eggs, one at a time, and beat the mixture until smooth. Spoon the pastry into a piping bag fitted with a plain nozzle and pipe swan neck shapes onto a baking sheet lined with baking paper.

On another lined baking sheet, spoon 2 teaspoons of pastry mix onto the sheet for each body. Dip your fingers in water, then shape the bodies. Bake the necks for approximately 5–8 minutes, and the bodies for approximately 15 minutes. Pierce the bodies to let the steam escape and return to the oven for another 3 minutes. Leave to set for a few minutes then place on a wire rack to go cold.

FILLING

Slice each body in half horizontally and place the baked edge face down. Beat the cream with the sugar in a bowl until the sugar is dissolved and the volume has increased. Fill each choux pastry body with cream. Place a neck at one end and fill with sliced strawberry. Slice the remaining body half in two lengthways and position as wings.

Lime Drizzle Cake with Lime Curd

MAKES 1 CAKE

SPONGE
180 g (6 oz) sugar
180 g (6 oz) margarine, softened
3 eggs, beaten
180 g (6 oz) self-raising (self-rising) flour
Zest of 1 lime
Juice of 2 limes, to drizzle
1 tablespoon icing (confectioners') sugar, to dust

LIME CURD
115 g (4 oz) sugar
25 g (1 oz) butter
2 eggs
Juice of 2 limes
Zest of 1 lime

Preheat the oven to 190°C/375°F/Gas mark 5. Grease and line two 20 cm (8 in) cake tins (pans).

SPONGE
In a large bowl, cream the sugar and margarine until soft and pale in colour. Mix in the eggs until well combined. Fold in the flour and lime zest. Divide the batter between the prepared tins and bake for 15–20 minutes. Leave to set in the tins for a few minutes then turn out onto a wire rack to go cold.

Cut the sponge in half. Mix the lime juice (for drizzling) with the icing sugar (for dusting) in a bowl and drizzle onto the top of the sponge.

LIME CURD
Meanwhile, to make the lime curd, in a heavy pan set over a medium heat, cook the sugar, butter, eggs and lime juice, whisking frequently, until it is thick enough to hold the marks of the whisk, about 12–15 minutes. Stir in the lime zest and leave to cool. Coat one cut side with lime curd and top with the remaining sponge half. Stamp out rounds using a cookie cutter, if you like.

BLAIR ATHOLL

Cheese and Pumpkin Seed Oatcakes with Smoked Salmon

MAKES 40–50

200 g (7 oz) fine oatmeal
200 g (7 oz) medium oatmeal
100 g (3½ oz) pinhead oatmeal, plus extra for dusting
1 teaspoon salt
1 teaspoon sugar
1 teaspoon baking powder

50 ml (2 fl oz) sunflower oil
500 ml (17 fl oz) boiling water
100 g (3½ oz) mature Cheddar cheese, grated (shredded)
80 g (2¾ oz) pumpkin seeds, flaked or lightly crushed
   and whole
Smoked salmon, to serve

Preheat the oven to 170°C/310°F/Gas mark 3½. Line several baking sheets with baking paper.

Mix all the dry ingredients together in a small electric mixer using a dough hook. Add the oil and water and mix for another 4 minutes until a very soft, workable paste has been formed. Dust the work surface with fine oatmeal, tip the paste onto it and leave to rest for a few minutes.

For plain oatcakes roll out the dough as it is. For flavoured oatcakes, add cheese and/or pumpkin seeds, flaked and whole. Roll out to no more than 5 mm (¼ in) and stamp out rounds with a 5 cm (2 in) cookie cutter. Bake for 30–40 minutes, until hard and crunchy. Leave to set for a few minutes, then turn out onto a wire rack to go cold. Top with smoked salmon just before serving.

Shortbread and Cranachan

SERVES 6

SHORTBREAD
150 g (5 oz) plain (all-purpose) flour, plus extra for dusting
130 g (4¼ oz) butter
20 g (¾ oz) cornflour (corn starch)
70 g (2¾ oz) caster (superfine) sugar

CRANACHAN
280 ml (9 fl oz) double (heavy) cream
1 tablespoon whiskey liqueur
250 g (9 oz) fresh raspberries
100 g (3½ oz) pinhead oatmeal, toasted

Preheat the oven to 180°C/350°F/Gas mark 4. Grease and line a baking tray.

SHORTBREAD
To make the shortbread, mix all the ingredients together in a large bowl until smooth. Roll out on a lightly floured surface until about 7 mm (generous ¼ in) thick. Stamp out 15 rounds using a cookie cutter. Bake for 10–16 minutes, or until light golden. Leave to cool for a few minutes, then turn out onto a wire rack to go cold. Store in an airtight container.

CRANACHAN
To make the cranachan, whip the cream until thick, but not stiff and stir in the whisky liqueur. Gently stir through the fresh raspberries. Divide between 6 espresso cups and decorate with toasted oatmeal just before serving. Serve with the shortbread.

Beer Sourdough Cheese and Pickle Sandwiches

MAKES 20 ROLLS

SOURDOUGH

400 g (14 oz) strong white bread flour
100 g (3½ oz) rye flour
10 g (⅓ oz) yeast
50 g (1¾ oz) sourdough starter (see Before You Begin)
250 ml (8 fl oz) beer or stout

10 g (⅓ oz) salt
Water

FILLING

Cheese, to fill
Pickle, to fill

SOURDOUGH

Mix the two flours together with the salt, yeast, sourdough and beer. Add water until you have a dough that is soft and elastic Leave, covered, to prove for 45 minutes then knock back (punch down), and leave to rise for another 45 minutes. Cut the dough into 20 equal rolls, shape them and leave to rest for 20 minutes. Shape the rolls again and leave to prove for 45 minutes. Bake in a hot oven at 240°C/450°F/Gas mark 8 for 45 minutes.

FILLING

Fill with cheese and pickle, as desired.

Sticky Toffee Puddings

MAKES 1 TRAY

SPONGE

175 g (6 oz) dried dates, diced
300 ml (½ pint) water
½ teaspoons bicarbonate of soda (baking soda)
175 g (6 oz) caster (superfine) sugar
2 eggs
90 g (3 oz) plain (all-purpose) flour
1 teaspoon baking powder
50 g (1¾ oz) butter, melted

TOFFEE SAUCE

200 g (7 oz) sugar
25 g (¾ oz) butter
50 ml (2 fl oz) whipping cream

Preheat the oven to 180°C/350°F/Gas mark 4. Lightly grease a 30 x 20 cm baking tray.

SPONGE

Put the dates and water in a large pan and bring to the boil over medium heat. When boiling, remove from the heat and add the bicarbonate of soda. Mix vigorously and allow to cool.

In a large bowl, beat the sugar and eggs until creamy. Add the sifted flour with the baking powder and fold gently. Pour in the melted butter and cooled date mixture and stir until combined. Pour into the prepared baking tin and bake for 45 minutes.

TOFFEE SAUCE

Meanwhile, to make the toffee sauce, pour the sugar into a saucepan and place over medium heat until caramelised and golden brown. Watch it carefully and stir continuously so that it doesn't catch. Remove from the heat and add the butter and cream. Stir until incorporated. Cut the pudding into squares and top with toffee sauce. Serve warm or cold.

WELSH BAKERY

Welsh Cakes

MAKES 24

CAKES

675 g (1½ lb) plain (all-purpose) flour, plus extra for dusting
15 g (½ oz) baking powder
225 g (8 oz) sugar
225 g (8 oz) butter, plus extra for cooking
3 small eggs
120 ml (¼ pint) milk
Handful of dried cranberries
Handful of candied orange

DECORATION

White chocolate, to dip
Icing (confectioners') sugar, to dust

CAKES

In a large bowl, mix the flour, baking powder and sugar until well combined. Rub in the butter with your fingertips until the mixture resembles fine breadcrumbs.

In a bowl, mix the eggs and milk and pour slowly into the flour mixture. Beat until a smooth dough has formed. Do not over-mix. Add the dried fruits and mix until combined. Roll out on a lightly floured surface to approximately 8 mm ($1/3$ in) thick, dusting the top of the dough and the surface regularly. Use a heart-shaped cutter to cut out the Welsh cakes. Cook on a lightly greased hotplate, or use a frying pan, until both sides are browned and the dough doesn't squidge out at the sides when pressed, 10 minutes. Set aside on paper towel to cool.

DECORATION

In a small bowl set over a pan of gently simmering water, melt the white chocolate. Dip one side of each cake in the chocolate. Dust the other half with icing sugar. Allow to cool before serving.

Mini Chocolate Éclairs

MAKES 10

CHOUX PASTRY
300 ml (½ pint) water
125 g (4½ oz) butter
180 g (6 oz) plain (all-purpose) flour
5 medium eggs

TOPPING AND FILLING
Milk chocolate, melted for topping
250 g (8 oz) fresh cream, for filling

Preheat the oven to 210°C/410°F/Gas mark 6½. Lightly grease two baking sheets.

CHOUX PASTRY
To make the choux pastry, heat the water and butter in a saucepan until the mixture comes to a boil. Remove from the heat, add the flour and beat until a thick and smooth paste. Let the mixture cool a little, then beat in the egg slowly. Put the mixture into a piping bag and pipe lengths directly onto a greased baking sheet. Bake for 20 minutes. Allow to cool slightly then turn out onto a wire rack to go cold.

TOPPING AND FILLING
Heat a small amount of milk chocolate in a bowl set over a pan of gently simmering water. Dip the top of each éclair into the chocolate. Allow to cool.

Cut each éclair to make an opening for the cream. Whisk the fresh cream in a large bowl, until it holds its shape. Part-fill a piping bag and pipe cream into the centre of each éclair.

BAKED IN TETTENHALL

Brummie Bacon Cakes

MAKES 8

4 rashers (strips) smoked streaky (fatty) bacon
225 g (8 oz) self-raising (self-rising) flour, plus extra for dusting
Pinch of salt
25 g (1 oz) butter
70 g (2½ oz) cheese, grated (shredded)

150 ml (¼ pint) milk
1 tablespoon tomato sauce
Dash of Worcestershire sauce
1 egg, beaten
Pork scratchings

CAKES

Grill (broil) the bacon until fairly crispy and leave to cool. Preheat the oven to 190°C/375°F/Gas mark 5. Line a baking sheet with baking paper. Sieve the flour and salt into a large bowl and rub in the butter until it resembles fine breadcrumbs. Cut the bacon into small pieces and stir into the flour mixture together with 50 g (1¾ oz) of the cheese.

In a small bowl, mix the milk, ketchup and Worcestershire sauce together and gradually mix into the flour mixture until it forms a rough ball of dough.

Roll out the pastry into a circle about 18 cm (7 in) diameter, divide into 8 equal triangles. Place on the prepared baking sheet. Brush the top of each with beaten egg. Chop the pork scratchings and scatter them on top of the triangles along with the remaining cheese. Bake for 20 minutes.

Asparagus Quiche

MAKES 4 TARTS

PASTRY

250 g (9 oz) plain (all-purpose) flour, plus extra for dusting
Pinch of salt
125 g (4½ oz) unsalted butter
1 egg
Water, to combine

FILLING

200 g (7 oz) asparagus
2 eggs
175 ml (6 fl oz) milk
175 ml (6 fl oz) double (heavy) cream
Pinch of salt and pepper
200 g (7 oz) hard sheep's milk cheese, grated (shredded)

Preheat the oven to 180°C/350°F/Gas mark 4.

PASTRY

To make the pastry, mix the flour, salt and butter in a blender until it resembles breadcrumbs. Add the egg and just enough water until the pastry comes together into a ball of dough. Wrap in cling film (plastic wrap) and refrigerate for 20 minutes.
Roll out the pastry on a lightly floured surface to 5 mm (¼ in) thick and cut out 4 circles slightly bigger than the tart tins (pans). Press a piece of pastry into each and trim around the edge. To blind bake the pastry cases, arrange a piece of baking paper on top of the pastry and fill with baking beans. Bake on a tray for 15 minutes, then remove the paper and beans and bake for another 4 minutes. Leave to cool.

FILLING

Cook the asparagus in a pan with a little water for a few minutes, or until tender. Leave to cool.

In a bowl, mix the eggs, milk, cream, salt and pepper. Put about four pieces of the asparagus into each pastry case, along with a small handful of the grated cheese. Pour the egg mixture into each case, leaving a little gap between the liquid and the top of the pastry. Bake for about 30 minutes or until the filling is set and the pastry is lightly browned around the edges.

Savoury Palmiers with Air-dried Ham and Perl Las Cheese

PASTRY
250 g (9 oz) strong white bread flour, plus extra for dusting
50 g (1¾ oz) spelt flour
¼ teaspoon baking powder
½ teaspoon salt
1 tablespoon olive oil
175 g (6 oz) unsalted butter, chilled and cut into small cubes
75 ml (2½ fl oz) milk
75 ml (2½ fl oz) water

FILLING
25 g (1 oz) mature Cheddar cheese, grated (shredded)
Freshly ground black pepper
25 g (1 oz) air-dried ham
25 g (1 oz) Perl Las blue cheese, crumbled
1 egg, beaten, for the egg wash

Preheat the oven to 220°C/425°F/Gas mark 7. Lightly grease a baking sheet.

PASTRY
To make the pastry, in a bowl pour the flours, baking powder and salt and mix until well combined. Add the olive oil and butter and rub in with your fingertips until the mixture resembles fine breadcrumbs. Add the milk and most of the water and stir to combine until the mixture comes together. Add more water if needed. Cover and chill for 20 minutes. Turn out onto a lightly floured surface and knead to combine slightly. Roll out the pastry to 40 x 20 cm (16 x 8 in). Fold into thirds, repeat and chill again. Repeat twice more at 30 minute intervals, chilling between rolling.

FILLING
Scatter the cheese on top of the pastry and a good grind of black pepper. Fold into thirds and re-roll to a square 20 x 20 cm (8 x 8 in). Cut it in half. Arrange the ham at intervals all along each strip. Sprinkle over the blue cheese. Fold each strip bringing the ends in to the centre and repeat. Cut into 5 mm (¼ in) strips with a sharp knife. Arrange cut-side up on the prepared baking sheets and brush with egg wash. Bake for 10 minutes, until golden.

Miller's Bread

MAKES 1 LOAF

BREAD DOUGH

500 g (1 lb 2 oz) wholemeal (whole-wheat) bread flour

320 ml (10 fl oz) water

10 g (¹/₃ oz) fresh yeast

1 teaspoon sea salt

2 teaspoons sunflower oil

165 g (5½ oz) pre-ferment (see Before You Begin)

50 g (1¾ oz) mixed pumpkin, sunflower, linseed and sesame
seeds

PRE-FERMENT

100 g (3½ oz) wholemeal (whole-wheat) flour

65 ml (2¼ fl oz) cold water

2 g fresh yeast

1 teaspoon salt

200g (7 oz) cream cheese, mixed with fennel or dill, to serve

200g (7 oz) smoked salmon, to serve

PRE-FERMENT

To make the pre-ferment, in a large bowl, mix all the ingredients to form a stiff dough and leave in a clean bowl covered with cling film (plastic wrap) overnight at room temperature.

BREAD DOUGH

To make the bread, combine all the ingredients, except the seeds, together in a bowl.

Add the seeds and fold evenly through the dough. Tip out onto a clean work surface. Without adding flour, fold and stretch the dough for at least 5 minutes. Leave to rest for 15 minutes in a covered bowl at room temperature. Tip out the dough onto the work surface. Flatten into a rectangular shape. Fold the top one-third over the centre third, then fold the remaining third over the centre. Turn the dough 90 degrees, flatten and repeat twice. Now roll the dough from the top towards you to make a log. Pinch along the side seams and the main seam. Pre-heat the oven to 220°C/425°F/Gas mark 7.

Place into a greased 900 g (2 lb) loaf tin (pan), seam side down. Leave covered with a clean dish towel and cling film (plastic wrap) for 30 minutes until your finger leaves an indentation on the dough when pressed.

Bake for 30–40 minutes, or until the loaf is golden on all sides. To serve, slice the bread, spread with cream cheese and top with smoked salmon.

THE COTTAGE KITCHEN

Devon Apple Cider Cake

MAKES 16

225 g (8 oz) sultanas (golden raisins)
150 ml (¼ pint) cider
225 g (8 oz) light brown sugar
180 g (6 oz) butter
2 eggs
290 g (10 oz) self-raising (self-rising) flour
1 teaspoon mixed (apple pie) spice
290 g (10 oz) cooking apples, peeled and chopped
85 g (3 oz) walnuts, chopped

Preheat the oven to 150°C/300°F/Gas mark 2. Grease and flour 16 cups of 2 x 12-cup muffin trays.

CAKE

Soak the sultanas in the cider and set aside. In a large bowl, cream the sugar and butter until light and fluffy. Slowly add the eggs, sifted flour and spice. Tip in the soaked sultanas and cider. Add the apples and mix through. Divide the batter equally between the cups, then scatter over the walnuts. Bake for 35 minutes, or until firm to the touch. Turn out onto a wire rack to go cool.

Chocolate and Orange Cheesecakes

MAKES 8

BISCUIT BASE
30 g (1 oz) butter
100 g (3½ oz) dark (bittersweet) chocolate digestives,
    finely crushed

FILLING
250 g (9 oz) cream cheese
75 ml (2½ fl oz) sour cream

100 g (3½ oz) caster (superfine) sugar
1 tablespoon plain (all-purpose) flour
½ teaspoon vanilla extract
Zest of 1 orange
1 large egg, separated

DECORATION
225 g (8 oz) plain (semi-sweet) chocolate

Line a 12-cup muffin tray (pan) with silicone paper.

BISCUIT BASE
Melt the butter in a pan set over medium heat. Remove from the heat and add the crushed biscuits. Stir to coat, then using a teaspoon, press some into each of the moulds, pressing down firmly.

Preheat the oven to 180°C/350°F/Gas mark 4.

FILLING
In a bowl, mix the cream cheese, sour cream, sugar, flour, vanilla, orange zest and egg yolk and whisk together until smooth.

In another bowl, whisk the egg white until soft peaks form. Using a large metal spoon, mix a spoonful of egg white into the cream cheese mixture, then stir through the rest. Divide the batter between the cups and bake for 15–20 minutes until lightly golden and firm to the touch. Leave to set in the tin for a few minutes, then turn out on to a wire rack to go cold. Chill.

DECORATION
Melt the chocolate in a heatproof bowl set over a pan of gently simmering water. Pour onto a baking sheet and leave to set. Refrigerate. Pull a large knife toward you across the chocolate to make curls. Arrange on top of chilled cheesecakes..

Sourdough Flatbread Stuffed with Pickled Cucumber and Blue Cheese

THE PHOENIX BAKERY

MAKES 4

FLAT BREAD
250 g (9 oz) strong white bread flour, plus extra for dusting
75 g (2½ oz) sourdough starter (*see Black Garlic and Scapes Sourdough recipe*)
75 ml (2½ fl oz) natural (plain) yogurt
75 ml (2½ fl oz) water
Pinch sea salt

PICKLED CUCUMBER
2 cucumbers
Salt
Apple cider vinegar
Blue-vein cheese, to serve

FLAT BREAD
To make the flat bread, tip the flour into a mixing bowl, make a well in the centre and add the starter, yogurt and water. Mix together gently. Cover and leave for 20 minutes. Add the salt with a splash of water, mix through again gently. Cover and refrigerate for 40 minutes. Fold your dough corner to corner while in the bowl. Cover with a clean dish towel, then repeat the refrigeration and folding process twice more.

Cut into 90 g (3 oz) pieces, shape into rounds and leave on a heavily floured table. Meanwhile, place a dry (20–25 cm) 8–10 in frying pan over heat on the stove top. Let it get smoking hot. Roll out each dough piece to the diameter of the pan. Place the bread in the pan and fry each side for 30 seconds. Repeat with the rest of the dough. Stack the baked bread and cover with a cloth.

PICKLED CUCUMBER
To make the pickled cucumber, skin two cucumbers, then slice into thin strips and place into a bowl. Sprinkle over some salt and pour over just enough cider vinegar to cover. Leave for 1 hour, to draw the moisture out. Drain off the excess liquid and brush off as much salt as you can. Cover and leave in the refrigerator until ready to use.

To assemble, arrange some of the cucumber across the centre of the flat bread and scatter over some cheese. Roll up to form a cigar shape. Trim off the ends and cut into three equal pieces. Serve fresh.

Double Strawberry tart with Balsamic and Mint

MAKES 4

PASTRY

90 g (3 oz) butter, softened
60 g (2 oz) caster (superfine) sugar
2 egg yolks
180 g (6 oz) plain (all-purpose) flour

FILLING AND GLAZE

15 g (½ oz) butter
12 strawberries
1 tablespoon balsamic vinegar
Mint sprigs, to decorate
Cream, to serve

Lightly grease four 7.5 cm (3 in) fluted loose-base tart tins (pans).

PASTRY

Cream the butter and sugar together in a large bowl and beat in the egg yolks. Mix in the flour until fully combined into a ball. Wrap in cling film (plastic wrap) and refrigerate for 30 minutes. Meanwhile, preheat the oven to 180°C/350°F/Gas mark 4.

Roll out the pastry to 5 mm (generous ⅛ in) thick, and use to line the tins. Line each pastry case with baking paper and fill with baking beans. Bake blind for 10 minutes, or until golden. Leave to cool on a wire rack to cool.

FILLING AND GLAZE

To make the strawberry and balsamic filling and glaze, in a pan, melt the butter over low heat. Meanwhile, cut 8 strawberries into quarters and place into the melted butter, cook for a couple of minutes until the fruit starts to fall. Add a generous splash of balsamic vinegar and cook on a low heat for 5 minutes – the mix will reduce slightly. Fill the tart cases with strawberry mixture saving some for a glaze.

Slice 1 strawberry per tart and feather over the top of the tart. Brush with the glaze and place a small sprig of fresh mint in the centre of each tart. Serve with cream.

Sweet Yorkshire Pudding with Ricotta, Chocolate and Cherries

DOLCIPANI ITALIAN BAKERY

MAKES 24

BATTER
400 g (14 oz) strong white bread flour
8 large eggs
100 g (3½ oz) icing (confectioners') sugar
Vanilla extract, in paste or the seeds of a pod (bean)
3 teaspoons cinnamon
400 ml (14 fl oz) cold milk
Glacé cherries, to decorate
100 g (3½ oz) apricot jam (jelly), to glaze
Vegetable oil, for greasing

FILLING
500 g (1 lb 2 oz) ricotta
300 g (11 oz) icing (confectioners') sugar
100 g (3½ oz) orange zest
3 teaspoons cinnamon
100 g (3½ oz) dark (bittersweet) chocolate,
  broken into chunks

FILLING
To make the filling, mix the ricotta and icing sugar together in a large bowl. Cover with cling film (plastic wrap) and chill for at least 1 hour, then press it through a fine sieve into a clean bowl. Mix in the rest of the ingredients until well combined. Use to part fill a piping bag fitted with a large smooth tip. Refrigerate until needed.

BATTER
In a large bowl, whisk the flour and eggs together until shiny. Add the icing sugar, vanilla and cinnamon. Slowly add the milk, whisking constantly, until you have a smooth, shiny batter.

Preheat the oven to 220°C/425°F/Gas mark 7. Add a drop of vegetable oil to alternate cups of several 12-cup muffin pans. Put the pans in the oven and when the oil is at smoking point, fill the greased cups to halfway, and immediately return it to the oven. Bake for 22 minutes without opening the oven or the cakes will collapse.

Fill the puddings from the top using the piping bag to insert the filling (they will have a hole at the top where you can see the hollow inside). Put half a cherry on top and brush the tops with apricot glaze. Serve hot or cold.

Ravazzata with Pork and Beef Ragu

MAKES 21

RAGU

60 ml (2 fl oz) olive oil
1 celery stalk, washed and sliced
1 carrot, peeled and chopped
2 garlic cloves, peeled and chopped
½ onion, peeled and chopped
300 g (11 oz) minced (ground) beef
300 g (11 oz) minced (ground) pork
125 ml (4 fl oz) Sicilian wine
400 g (14 oz) can Italian diced tomatoes
1 tablespoon tomato purée (passata)
100 g (3½ oz) frozen peas

2 bay leaves
2 teaspoons salt
300 g (11 oz) Pecorino cheese with peppercorns
1 egg, beaten
7 tablespoons sesame seeds

BRIOCHE

1 kg (2 lb 4 oz) '00' Italian flour
100 g (3½ oz) granulated (white) sugar
100 g (3½ oz) lard
50 g (1¾ oz) fresh yeast
500 ml (17 fl oz) tepid water
20 g (¾ oz) salt

RAGU

To make the ragu, heat the olive oil in a large frying pan set over a medium heat, then fry the celery, carrot, garlic and onion until golden. Add the beef and pork mince and fry until cooked through. Add the wine and let it evaporate. Add the tomatoes, tomato purée and peas and bay leaves. Bring the mixture to a boil, then reduce the heat and simmer for about 2 hours. Towards the end of the simmering time, season with salt.

BRIOCHE

To make the brioche, mix the flour, sugar, lard and yeast together in a bowl using an electric mixer fitted with a dough hook until well combined. Add the salt and then drizzle in the water. Mix until the dough leaves the sides of the bowl. Cover and leave in a warm place to double in volume, about 1 hour.

Divide the dough into 120 g (4 oz) portions. Form into balls, then flatten them into rounds about 15 cm (6 in) diameter. Put a large spoonful of ragu in the centre and add four or five cubes of cheese. Close the pastries as if a parcel and turn them upside down. Brush with beaten egg and sprinkle with sesame seeds. Leave to prove in a warm place for about 15 minutes. Meanwhile, preheat the oven to 200°C/400°F/Gas mark 6. Lightly grease two baking sheets. Place the pastries on the prepared sheet and bake for about 12 minutes.

Rye Bread Open Sandwich with Smoked Trout and Nettle Salsa

MAKES 1 LOAF

RYE BREAD
250 g (9 oz) rye flour, plus extra for dusting
200 ml (7 fl oz) warm water
1 teaspoon salt
250 g (9 oz) rye sour starter (*see Before You Begin*)
Oil, for greasing

FILLING
1 smoked trout
100 g (3½ oz) cream cheese

SALSA VERDE
Handful of fresh mint
Handful of fresh basil
Handful (gloved) of young nettle tops
15 g (½ oz) fresh parsley
2 pickled gherkins
1 tablespoon capers
3 garlic cloves
4 anchovies
1 tablespoon mustard
6 tablespoons olive oil
1 tablespoon red wine vinegar
Juice of 1 lemon
Salt and pepper

Grease and dust with flour 3 mini loaf tins.

RYE BREAD
To make the rye bread, combine the rye flour with the water and salt in a large bowl and mix to combine. Add the sourdough starter and mix to combine. With wet hands, split the dough between the prepared tins. Push the dough flat then dust with rye flour. Place a dish towel over the tins and prove in a warm place for 2 hours.

Preheat the oven to 240°C/475°F/Gas mark 9. Put the tins into a preheated oven then immediately reduce the oven temperature to 220°C/425°F/Gas mark 7 and bake for 20–30 minutes.

SALSA VERDE
To make the salsa verde, finely chop all the ingredients, then mix together in a large bowl.

FILLING
To serve, slice the rye bread, spread with cream cheese, top with smoked trout and some salsa verde.

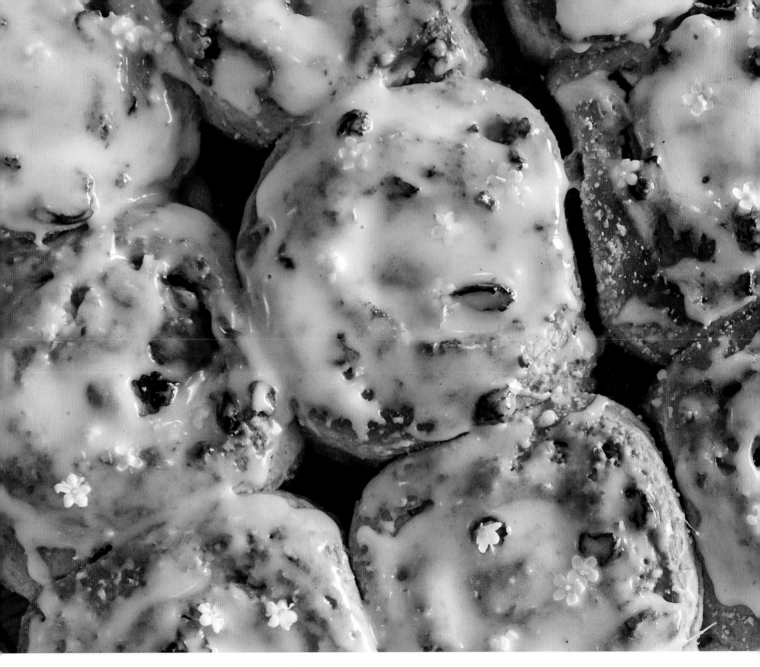

Iced Ale Bun

. . . .

MAKES 12

SPONGE

200 g (7 oz) strong white bread flour
20 g (¾ oz) fresh yeast
270 ml (7 ¾ fl oz) ale

DOUGH

100 g (3½ oz) wholemeal (whole-wheat) flour
200 g (7 oz) strong white bread flour, plus extra for dusting
10 g (¾ oz) salt
75 g (2½ oz) sugar
75 g (2½ oz) butter, diced

1 egg, beaten
30 g (1 oz) butter
100 g (3½ oz) mixed raisins and diced apples, soaked in
   100 ml (3½ fl oz) ale
1 teaspoon mixed (apple pie) spice
1 tablespoon sugar
35 g (1¼ oz) round almonds (almond meal)
Zest of 1 orange

GLAZE

5 tablespoons icing (confectioners') sugar
1 tablespoon hot water

SPONGE

Put the flour and yeast in a bowl and rub in with your fingertips. Warm the ale slightly in a pan set over low heat. Whisk the ale into the ingredients, cover and leave to bubble for 45 minutes. Pour the sponge into a mixer fitted with a dough hook.

DOUGH

Add the flours, salt and sugar to the sponge. Start the mixer on a slow speed, until the ingredients come together to form a dough. Add the diced butter a piece at a time so as not to make the dough greasy. Speed up the mixer and mix for another 6–7 minutes. Cover and set the dough aside to prove for 1 hour in a warm place until risen.

Tip the dough out onto a lightly floured surface and roll out to a square 40 x 36 cm (16 x 14 in). Paint a line of beaten egg along one long edge. This will form the seal when the dough is rolled up. Melt a small amount of butter in a pan and paint all over the surface of the dough. Drain the ale from the fruit and spread the fruit evenly over the buttered surface. Sprinkle with mixed spice, sugar and ground almonds. Beginning from the top, roll the dough into a sausage shape, pushing it against the egg side to seal. Trim off the ends. Brush melted butter all over the sausage shape. Cut into 12 equal pieces. Place close together on a lined baking sheet. Cover and prove for 45–60 minutes.

Preheat the oven to 210°C/410°F/Gas mark 6½. Bake for 16 minutes. Turn out onto a wire rack.

GLAZE

To make the glaze, put the icing sugar and hot water in a bowl and mix together until smooth. Use to glaze the hot buns. Set aside to cool before serving.

Orange Shortbread Fingers with Lavender Sugar and Raspberry Coulis

MAKES 15 FINGERS

SHORTBREAD
125 g (4½ oz) butter
55 g (2 oz) caster (superfine) sugar
180 g (6 oz) plain (all-purpose) flour, plus extra for dusting
Zest of 1 unwaxed orange
Lavender sugar (see tip), for sprinkling

RASPBERRY COULIS
150 g (5 oz) sugar
500 g (1 lb 2 oz) raspberries
120 ml (4 fl oz) water

Preheat the oven to 190°C/375°F/Gas 5.

SHORTBREAD
To make the shortbread, beat the butter and sugar together in a large bowl until smooth. Add the orange zest, then stir in the flour until a smooth paste forms. Do not over-mix the batter. Tip out onto a lightly floured work surface and gently roll out to 1 cm (³/₈ in) thick. Cut into fingers. Cover and chill for 20 minutes.

Bake for 15–20 minutes, or until pale golden-brown. Set aside on a wire rack to cool. Dust with lavender sugar.

RASPBERRY COULIS
To make the raspberry coulis, combine the ingredients in a saucepan and bring to a boil over medium-high heat. Reduce the

heat to low and continue to cook until the sugar is dissolved, about 8 minutes. Use a pastry brush dipped in water to brush down any sugar crystals on the side of the pan. Remove from the heat and leave to go cold. Pour into a blender and purée until smooth. Pass through a fine-meshed sieve and discard the seeds. Serve as a dessert with ice cream and coulis.

Tip: To make lavender sugar, 1 teaspoon of lavender flowerhead with 500 g (1 lb 2 oz) of sugar and store in a dry, airtight container for 1 week prior to using.

Brandy Snap with Lemon Cream

MAKES 8

BRANDY SNAP

55 g (2 oz) butter

55 g (2 oz) demerara (raw) sugar

55 g (2 oz) golden (light corn) syrup

50 g (1¾ oz) plain (all-purpose) flour

½ teaspoon ground ginger

½ teaspoon lemon juice

100 g (3½ oz) milk chocolate, melted

CREAM FILLING

100 g (3¾ oz) mascarpone

200 g (7 oz) whipping cream

20 g (¾ oz) icing (confectioners') sugar

Zest of 2 lemons

Preheat the oven to 180°C/350°F/Gas 4. Grease several baking sheets.

BRANDY SNAP

Heat the butter, sugar and syrup gently in a small, heavy pan over gentle heat until the sugar has dissolved. Don't let the mixture boil. Leave to cool slightly, then sieve in the flour and ginger. Pour in the lemon juice and mix vigorously. Drop 4 heaped teaspoonfuls of the mixture onto the prepared baking sheets, spacing them well apart and forming them into circles. Bake for 10–15 minutes, or until the mixture is well spread out, a dark golden colour and has a popped bubble appearance. Let the shapes cool a little, then lift from the baking parchment using a palette knife. Working quickly roll the warm mixture around a cream horn case. Press the join lightly together to seal, and leave to firm up. When cool dip in melted chocolate.

CREAM FILLING

Using an electric mixer, whip the mascarpone with the cream and sugar until thick like firmly whipped crream. Gently fold in the lemon zest and chill until required.

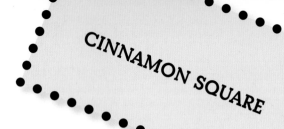
CINNAMON SQUARE

Leeks, Gruyère, Watercress in Pastry

MAKES 28

CHOUX PASTRY
75 g (2½ oz) butter
150 ml (¼ pint) water
95 ml (3¼ fl oz) milk
115 g (4 oz) strong white bread flour
2 eggs, beaten
70 g (2¼ oz) Gruyère cheese, grated (shredded)
1 tablespoon chopped chives
Pinch of salt

FILLING
100 g (3½ oz) butter
6 medium leeks
2 bunches spring onions (scallions), finely chopped
1 large bunch watercress, finely chopped
2 generous pinches of nutmeg
salt and freshly ground black pepper
6 egg yolks
120 g (4 oz) Gruyere cheese, finely grated (shredded)
200 g (7 oz) crème frâiche

Preheat the oven to 200°C/400°F/Gas mark 6. Line two baking sheets with baking paper.

CHOUX PASTRY
Put the butter, water and milk in a saucepan over a medium heat and bring to the boil. Remove from the heat and immediately add the flour, stir thoroughly. Return to a low heat for a minute to cook, stirring continuously until the mixture comes away from the sides of the pan. Leave to cool. Add the egg, a little at a time, beating well until the mixture is smooth. Stir in the cheese, chives and a pinch of salt. Use to part fill a piping bag. Pipe 20g (¾ oz) balls onto the prepared baking sheets, spacing them well apart. Bake for 25 minutes, until crisp. Leave to set for a few minutes, then turn out onto a wire rack to cool.

FILLING
Melt the butter in a large saucepan. Sweat the leeks over a low heat, covered, for up to 20 minutes until very soft. Stir occasionally, and ensure they do not brown. Add the spring onions, watercress, nutmeg, salt and pepper. Stir thoroughly and remove from the heat. Leave to cool.

Whisk together the egg yolks and crème fraiche in a microwave-proof jug. Heat gently in a microwave to thicken. Start with a couple of 30 second bursts, stirring with the whisk after each, then finish off with 10 second bursts, until the sauce has thickened but is not overcooked. Stir in the cheese. Add the sauce to the cooled leek mixture and stir thoroughly. Cover and chill.

Cut the top off each choux ball. Fill generously using a piping bag. Replace top and garnish with a sprig of watercress.

Macchiato

MAKES 4

MACCHIATO

1 small egg, plus 4 large egg yolks, beaten
40 g (1½ oz) caster (superfine) sugar
250 ml (9 fl oz) whipping cream
115 ml espresso
90 g (3 oz) plain (semi-sweet) chocolate, melted

FOAM

1½ large egg whites
¾ gelatine leaf
1 tablespoon water
Unsweetened cocoa powder, to finish

Preheat the oven to 190°C/375° /Gas mark 5. Prepare a bain marie by part filling a large heatproof tray with water.

MACCHIATO

Whisk the eggs and sugar together in a large jug. Heat the cream in a saucepan over medium heat until nearly boiling. Remove from the heat, and add slowly to the jug, whisking to combine. Add the espresso and melted chocolate. Stir thoroughly. Pass through a sieve. Pour 50g (1¾ oz) into each espresso cup. Set each cup in the bain marie. Top up the bain marie if necessary, so the water is level with the mixture. Bake for 30 minutes, or until set. Allow to cool then place in the refrigerator.

FOAM

Whisk the egg whites until stiff. Soften the gelatine in water, then heat gently in microwave to dissolve. Fold carefully through the egg whites. Top macchiatos with foam, and return to the fridge to set. Dust with cocoa powder before serving.

Boston Brown Bread with Cream Cheese and Pickled Grapes

OUTSIDER TART

MAKES 1

TEABREAD

240 ml (7¾ fl oz) buttermilk

80 g (3 oz) molasses (black treacle)

4 tablespoons canola oil, plus extra for greasing

100 g (3½ oz) wholemeal (whole-wheat) flour

75 g (2½ oz) plain (all-purpose) flour

50 g (1¾ oz) yellow cornmeal or polenta

4 tablespoons, soft dark brown sugar

1 teaspoon bicarbonate of soda (baking soda)

½ teaspoon salt

90 g (3¼ oz) dark raisins

90 g (3¼ oz) sultanas (golden raisins)

60 g (2 oz) pecans or walnuts, chopped

FILLING

Cream cheese

Pickled grapes

Preheat the oven to 180ºC/350ºF/Gas mark 4. Grease and line a 23 x 12 cm (9 x 5 in) loaf tin (pan).

TEABREAD

In a large mixing bowl, combine the buttermilk, molasses and canola oil. In a medium mixing bowl, whisk together the flours, cornmeal, sugar, baking soda and salt until evenly combined. Make a well in the middle and pour in the wet ingredients. Stir until nearly mixed, then add in the dried fruit and nuts, and stir a few more times to blend them in. Don't over-mix the batter; if small traces of flour are still visible that's perfect. Tip into the prepared tin. Bake in the centre of the oven for 40–45 minutes, or until a skewer emerges clean from the centre. It will be dark golden in colour and spring back when touched. Leave to cool in the tin for about 15 minutes before turning out onto a wire rack to go cold. The longer the bread cools, the cleaner the slice will be.

FILLING

Top the slices with cream cheese and pickled grapes.

Tip: Typically Boston Brown Bread is steamed in a coffee can but, for speed, we came up with this quick bread as a great alternative. We found green raisins, which we are obsessed with but you can use any combination of raisins, sultanas and currants.

Delta Jelly Sandwich

MAKES 1

125 g (4½ oz) unsalted butter, melted, plus extra for greasing
500 ml (16 fl oz) double (heavy) cream
2 large eggs
250 g (9 oz) plain (all-purpose) flour
115 g (4 oz) coarse cornmeal
150 g (5 oz) sugar

4½ teaspoons baking powder
½ teaspoon salt
275 g (10 oz) berry jam

Preheat the oven to 200°C/400°F/Gas mark 6. Grease and line a 20 x 20 cm (8 x 8 in) tin (pan).

TEABREAD

In the bowl of an electric mixer fitted with a paddle, combine the melted butter, cream and eggs. On low speed, slowly add the flour, cornmeal, sugar, baking powder and salt until the ingredients are just combined and not lumpy. Tip into the prepared tin. Put in oven and immediately reduce the oven temperature to 180°C/350°F/Gas mark 4. Bake for 45–50 minutes, or until lightly browned. The cornbread should spring back when touched and a small skewer should emerge clean. Allow to cool completely. Remove from the baking tray. Slice into wedges. Cut each wedge in half and fill with jam. Reassemble and spread jam on top.

Tip: This batter can be made and refrigerated in a covered container for up to 3 days. Add 3–5 minutes to the baking time to compensate for the chilled batter.

Lavender Shortbreads with Raspberries and Mascarpone

THE CAKE SHOP BAKERY

SHORTBREAD

100 g caster (superfine) sugar, plus extra for dusting

1 teaspoon crushed lavender, plus extra for dusting

Pinch of salt

300 g plain (all-purpose) flour

250 g butter, chilled and diced

FILLING

Small tub of mascarpone

Zest of 1 lemon

2 tablespoons lemon juice

2 tablespooons icing (confectioners') sugar

Raspberries, to decorate

Preheat the oven to 180°C/350°F/Gas mark 4. Grease a baking sheet

SHORTBREADS

Mix all the shortbread ingredients in an electric mixer. Add the butter all at once and mix until a dough forms. Roll out on a lightly floured surface to 7 mm (¼ in) thick and stamp out rounds using a cookie cutter. Bake for 15–20 minutes until the edges are just starting to turn borwn. Dust with caster sugar and lavender.

FILLING

Mix the filling ingredients together until smooth. Adjust the lemon or icing as desired. Top each shortbread round and finish with 4 rapsberries.

Smoked Duck and Cherry Jam Sandwich

MAKES 2 LOAVES

BREAD
600 g (1 lb 6 oz) strong white bread flour
15 g (½ oz) salt
400 ml (14 fl oz) cold water
20 g (¾ oz) fresh yeast

FILLING
Rainbow chard
Cherry chutney
Smoked duck
Butter, for spreading
Cherries, to decorate

BREAD
Put the flour and salt into a bowl and mix thoroughly. In a small bowl, mix together the water and yeast until the yeast dissolves then add to the flour and salt mixture. Mix until everything is combined. Cover with a damp cloth and leave for 20–30 minutes. Tip out the dough on to a lightly floured work surface and knead for at least 30 minutes. Put in a clean bowl, cover with a damp cloth and leave for 60 minutes in a warm place. Turn out onto a lightly floured surface and fold the dough in half one-way and then the other way to aid the development of the structure. Return the dough to the bowl for another 30 minutes. Cut into equal portions and place each in a baking tin (pan). In a warm place, prove small rolls for 20 minutes for a large loaf for 40 minutes. It is ready when you touch the dough and the indentation disappears. Bake at 220°C/425°F/Gas mark 7 for 40–60 minutes.

FILLING
Slice the bread, spread with butter, then the duck. Top with chutney and chard. Remove the crusts and cut into fingers. Top with a cherry, to decorate.

Earl Grey Mille Feuille

MAKES 10

PASTRY CREAM

500 ml (17 fl oz) milk
1 heaped teaspoon Earl Grey loose leaf tea
40 g (1¼ oz) cornflour (corn starch)
115 g (4 oz) caster (superfine) sugar
2 eggs
¼ teaspoon salt
55 g (2 oz) unsalted butter, cubed

TO DECORATE

225 g (8 oz) strawberries, thinly sliced
Icing (confectioners') sugar, for dusting
10 hazelnuts on wooden skewers
30 g (1 oz) caster (superfine) sugar

PASTRY

500 g (1 lb 2 oz) puff pastry, baked according to the
  manufacturer's instructions

PASTRY CREAM

Pour the milk into a saucepan. Tie the loose-leaf tea in a square of muslin and add to the milk. Place over a medium heat and bring almost to the boil, stirring occasionally. Remove from the heat, cover and leave to infuse for a few minutes. Squeeze the muslin bag to extract the tea. Return the milk to the heat and bring almost to the boil, stirring occasionally.
Meanwhile, in a bowl, whisk together the cornflour, sugar, eggs and salt.

Add one-third of the hot milk to the egg mix, while whisking continuously until combined, then pour the egg mix back into the pan with the rest of the milk. Whisk continuously over a medium heat until the mixture thickens. As the first boiling bubbles appear, remove from heat and add the butter in stages, whisking between each addition. Tip into a heatproof container, directly cover the surface with cling film (plastic wrap), so that a skin doesn't form. Cool, then refrigerate until chilled.

TO DECORATE

Carefully cut the pastry into rectangles (you need 3 per pastry). Part-fill a piping bag fitted with an 8 mm (¼ in) nozzle with the pastry cream. Onto the first pastry layers, pipe dots of pastry cream then add a layer of strawberries. Top with a second layer of pastry and repeat. Place the third layer of pastry on top and drench with icing sugar. Heat a metal skewer over a naked flame and brand the design of your choice into the icing sugar. Pipe a dot of pastry cream on one end of the mille feuille

To make the hazelnut shards, heat the caster sugar in a saucepan over medium heat. Do not stir. Swirl the pan only until the sugar turns a deep colour. Dip the skewered hazelnuts in the caramel and then allow to hang off the side of the table to produce shards. Anchor them with a heavy implement. When set, use to top the mille feuille.

Where to Find Britain's Best Bakeries

1066 BAKERY
Bank Buildings
Station Road
Hastings
East Sussex
TN34 1NG
Tel: 01424 437007

CLERVAUX CAFE
38 Coniscliffe Road
Darlington
DL3 7RG
Tel: 01325 351 879

APPLEBY BAKERY
Appleby-in-Westmorland
24 Boroughgate
Appleby-In-Westmorland
Cumbria
CA16 6XB
Tel: 01768 351667

BAKED IN TETTENHALL
1 Upper Green
Wolverhampton
West Midlands
WV6 8QQ
Tel: 07868 738367

BAKERY ANDANTE
352 Morningside Rd
Edinburgh
Midlothian
EH10 4QL
Tel: 0131 447 8473

BECWS MEFUS
Talwrn Road
Llangefni
Isle of Anglesey
LL77 7RP
Tel: 01248 722 564

BIRDHOUSE BAKERY
33 Drummond St
Crieff
Perthshire
PH5 2AN
Tel: 01764 681424

BIRDWOOD BAKERY
125 Leigh Rd
Leigh-on-Sea
Essex
SS9 1JH
Tel: 01702 480404

BLAIR ATHOLL WATERMILL & TEAROOM
Blair Atholl
Pitlochry
Perthshire
PH18 5SH
Tel: 01796 481321

BLUE FUCHSIA
8 New St
Ledbury
Herefordshire
HR8 2DX
01531 635224

BOULANGERIE JADE
44 Tranquil Vale
Blackheath
London
SE3 0BD
Tel: 020 8318 1916

BURBIDGE'S BAKERY
155 Weyhill Rd
Andover
Hampshire
SP10 3BH
Tel: 01264 364800

CAKE BOX
76 Wessex Rd
Yeovil
Somerset
BA21 3LR
Tel: 01935 421453

CARACOLI
15 Broad St
Alresford
Hampshire
SO24 9AR
Tel: 01962 738730

168 High St
Guildford
GU1 3HS
Tel: 01483 346060

100 High Street
Winchester
Hampshire
SO23 9AH
Tel: 01962 808185

CHAMPS BAKERY

19 Oxford St
Whitstable
CT5 1DB
Tel: 01227 273189

CINNAMON SQUARE

9 Church St
Rickmansworth
Hertfordshire
WD3 1BX
Tel: 01923 778353

CISSY GREEN'S BAKERY

30 Deardengate
Haslingden
Rossendale
Lancashire
BB4 5QJ
Tel: 01706 215099

CLOUD 9 BAKERY

15 Brighton Pl
Brighton
BN1 1HJ
Tel: 01273 723020

COCORICO PÂTISSERIE

Niazs House
53–55 Whitchurch Rd
Cardiff
South Glamorgan
CF14 3JP
Tel: 02921 328177

CORNFIELD BAKERY

76 High St
Wheatley
Oxford
OX33 1XP
Tel: 01865 872682

CORRISTER & WHITE

45 Hill Road
Clevedon
North Somerset
BS21 7PD
Tel: 01275 871361

COWBURN'S FAMILY BAKERY

32 Buxton Road
Stockport
Cheshire
SK6 8BH
Tel: 01663 763337

CRAGS COUNTRY BAKERY

29 Botchergate
Carlisle
Cumbria
CA1 1RZ
Tel: 01228 401110

DENVER MILLS

Hanse House
S Quay
Kings Lynn
Norfolk
PE30 5GN
Tel: 01553 760673

DOLCIPANI ITALIAN BAKERY

High St
Town Centre
Devizes
Wiltshire
SN10 1AT
Tel: 01380 728941

EAST AND WEST BAKERY

1 Butchers Row
Barnstaple
Devon
EX31 1BW
Tel: 01271 377577

ELIZABETH MAY

40 Lyons Lane
Chorley
Lancashire
PR6 0PJ
Tel: 07927 169146

FROST AND SNOW

Midland Heart's
The Snow Hill:
86 Old Snow Hill
Birmingham
B4 6GD
0845 603 6166

GARVALD BAKERY

600 Gorgie Road
Edinburgh
EH11 3AL
0131 516 2771

GATINEAU

209 Banbury Road
Sumertown
Oxford
OX2 7HQ
Tel: 01865 311779

JEANETTE'S CAKERY

58A–60 Bingley Rd
Shipley
Saltaire
West Yorkshire
BD18 4SD
Tel: 01274 921902

LAWTON'S PIES LTD

74 Derby Street
Leek
Staffordshire, ST7 3PG
Tel: 01538 383166

LILIBETS OF PARIS

24 Stanley St
Town Centre
Southport
PR9 0BY
Tel: 01704 536001

MAD HATTERS

49 Bridge Street Row E
Chester
Cheshire
CH1 1NW
Tel: 01244 323444

MAISON MAYCI

8 Poplar Road
Kings Heath
Birmingham
B14 7AD
0121 444 8167

148 Alcester Road
Moseley
Birmingham
B13 8HS
0121 449 4413

MR BUN THE BAKER

12 Sandford Avenue
Church Stretton
Shropshire
SY6 6BW
Tel: 01694 723018

MURRAYS

114 South St
Perth
PH2 8PA
Tel: 01738 624633

ORIGINAL BAKEHOUSE

16–17 St Marys Green
Whickham
Newcastle-upon-Tyne
Tyne and Wear
NE16 4DN
Tel: 0191 420 0592

OUTSIDER TART

83 Chiswick High Rd
Chiswick
London
W4 2EF
Tel: 0207 096 1609

SEEDS 2 BAKERY

35 High St
Totnes
Devon
TQ9 5NP
Tel: 01803 862526

SPONDON BAKERY

7 Moor St
Derby
DE21 7EA
Tel: 01332 678366

ST MARY'S BAKERY

4 St Marys Street
Brecon
Powys
LD3 7AA
Tel: 01874 624311

SWEETHART COFFEE & CAKE

10 Derwent Street
Consett
County Durham
DH8 8LU
Tel: 01207 501100

THE ANGEL'S SHARE

Richmond Station
Station Yard
Richmond
North Yorkshire
DL10 4LD
Tel: 01748 828 261

THE BAKERS' TABLE

The Mill/The Square
Brecon
LD3 0BW
Tel: 01874 711125

THE CAKE SHOP BAKERY

21 Thoroughfare
Woodbridge
Suffolk
IP12 1AA
Tel: 01394 382515

THE COTTAGE KITCHEN

28A Fore St
Kingsbridge
Devon
TQ7 1NY
Tel: 01548 852456

THE MUFFIN TOP BOUTIQUE BAKERY

29 Duke St
Whitehaven
Cumbria
CA28 7EU
Tel: 01946 591503

THE PHOENIX BAKERY

6-7 Coburg Place
Weymouth
Dorset
DT4 8HP
01305 767894

THE PUDDING ROOM

Hognaston Bypass
Nr Carsington Water
Ashbourne
Derbyshire
DE6 1NQ

THE SANDWICH BOX

3 Imperial Square
Cheltenham
Gloucestershire
GL50 1QB
Tel: 01242 230831

THE SUNFLOWER BAKERY

40 High Street
Dore
Sheffield
S17 3GU

THE VINTAGE CAKE HOUSE

5 Downing St
Farnham
GU9 7PB
Tel: 01252 728254

THE WEE BOULANGERIE

67 Clerk St
Edinburgh
Midlothian
EH8 9JG
Tel: 0131 629 3134

VERA'S TRADITIONAL CARIBBEAN BAKERY

Old Walsall Road
Birmingham
BA2 1NR

VICTORIA BAKERY

83 High St
Barnet
Hertfordshire
EN5 5UR
Tel: 0208 449 0790

WELSH BAKERY

45 Old Bridge
Haverfordwest
Dyfed
SA61 2EZ
Tel: 01437 762981

YASAR HALIM PÂTISSERIE

495–497 Green Lanes
Haringey
London
N4 1AL
Tel: 0208 340 8090

YE OLDE PASTIE SHOPPE

31 Churchgate
Bolton
Lancashire
BL1 1HU
Tel: 01204 524834

Index

• •

ACKNOWLEDGEMENTS

With thanks to the judges Mich Turner and Peter Sidwell;
Kate Ward and Katy Herbert of Shine TV; and
David Christopher, Frances Adams, Lisa O'Connell and Claire
Burton of Shine 360; and David Cotter.

The publishers would like to thank the following for use of
their images: Alamy: Page 182. Cinnamon Square: Page
158 top left and 345 bottom. Fotolia: Page 17 bottom, 23,
29 top, 64 top centre and bottom left, 65 bottom centre, 67
top, 75, 85, 107 top, 111 top centre and left centre, 113,
129 top, 141, 147 top, 159 bottom centre, 159 top centre,
173 top, 197 top, 205 top, 208 top centre, 209 bottom
centre and top centre, 215 top, 219 top, 223 top, 233 top,
243 top, 247 top, 251 top and 262. Gatineau: Page 244.
Lawton's Pies: Page 87 bottom. Lilibets of Paris: Page 42.
Shutterstock: Page 13, 16 top, 16 centre right, 37, 58, 61,
87 top, 100, 110 bottom centre, 117, 133 top, 141, 155
top, 158 bottom left, 167 left, 181 top, 191 top, 212, 227
top, 232, 252, 301 and 315. The Wee Boulangerie: Page 25.
Murrays: Page 27. Mad Hatters: Page 54. The Bakers' Table:
Page 122

First published in 2014 by
New Holland Publishers
London • Sydney • Cape Town • Auckland
www.newhollandpublishers.com

The Chandlery Unit 114 50 Westminster Bridge Road London SE1 7QY
1/66 Gibbes Street Chatswood NSW 2067 Australia
Wembley Square First Floor Solan Road Gardens Cape Town 8001 South Africa
218 Lake Road Northcote Auckland New Zealand

A catalogue record of this book is available at the British Library

ISBN: 9781742575124

10 9 8 7 6 5 4 3 2 1

Publisher: Fiona Schultz
Editors: Simona Hill and Jodi De Vantier
Designer: Tracy Loughlin
Home ecconomist: Sharon Kennedy
Stylist: Arum Shim
Photographers: David Cotter and Sue Stubbs
Production director: Olga Dementiev
Printer: Toppan Leefung Printing Limited

Follow New Holland Publishers on
Facebook: www.facebook.com/NewHollandPublishers